Aim high in the KS2 SATS with CGP!

This CGP book is packed with SATS-style Maths questions split up into short, sharp tests. It's a brilliant way to help pupils prepare for the real tests in Year 6!

These Advanced Level tests cover every topic they'll need for a top mark in the SATS. We've even included Arithmetic Tests to match the latest curriculum perfectly.

Plus — all the answers are included in a cut-out-and-keep section!

What CGP is all about

Our sole aim here at CGP is to produce the highest quality books — carefully written, immaculately presented and dangerously close to being funny.

Then we work our socks off to get them out to you — at the cheapest possible prices.

Contents

Set A

Test 1 1
Test 2 4
Test 3 7
Test 4 10
Test 5 13
Arithmetic Test 16
Scoresheet 18

Set B

Test 1 19
Test 2 22
Test 3 25
Test 4 28
Test 5 31
Arithmetic Test 34
Scoresheet 36

Set C

Test 1 37
Test 2 40
Test 3 43
Test 4 46
Test 5 49
Arithmetic Test 52
Scoresheet 54

Answers 55
Progress Chart 63

Just like in the real tests, calculators are not allowed.

Published by CGP
Editors: Liam Dyer, Rob Harrison, Shaun Harrogate
With thanks to Alison Griffin and Simon Little for the proofreading.

ISBN: 978 1 78294 681 6
Clipart from Corel®
Printed by Elanders Ltd, Newcastle upon Tyne.
Based on the classic CGP style created by Richard Parsons.

Text, design, layout and original illustrations © Coordination Group Publications Ltd. (CGP) 2016
All rights reserved.

**Photocopying this book is not permitted. Extra copies are available from CGP with next day delivery.
0800 1712 712 • www.cgpbooks.co.uk**

Set A: Test 1

There are **8 questions** in this test. Give yourself **10 minutes** to answer them all.

1. Round 378 746:

   to the nearest hundred

   to the nearest thousand

   1 mark

2. Fill in the missing number in the calculation below.

   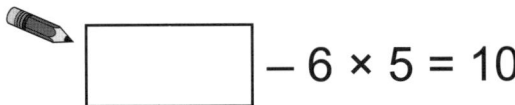 − 6 × 5 = 10

   1 mark

3. Ralph has cut a triangle from a piece of card, as shown below. What is the area of the triangle?

   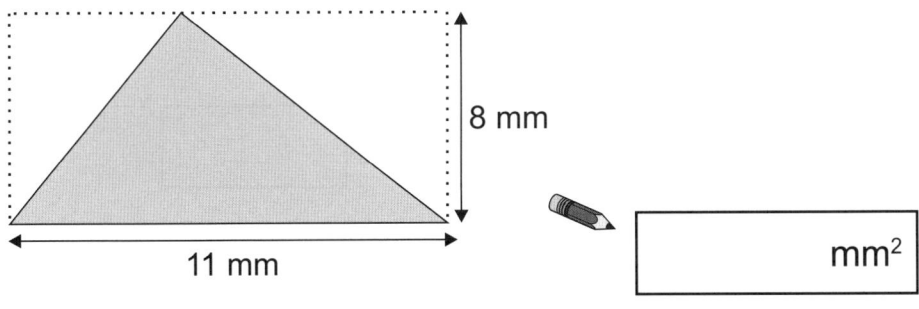 mm²

   1 mark

4. Circle the values which are equivalent to $\frac{3}{4}$.

$\frac{9}{12}$ 0.4 $\frac{1}{2}$ 0.75 $\frac{4}{5}$

1 mark

5. Two pots of jam weigh 120 g in total.
How much will five pots of jam weigh?

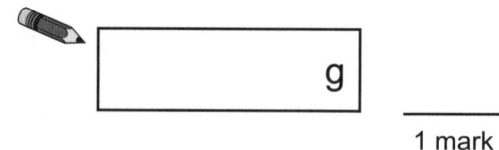
g

1 mark

6. Write down the rule for this number sequence.

2.5,   5,   7.5,   10...

1 mark

Write down the next three terms in the sequence.

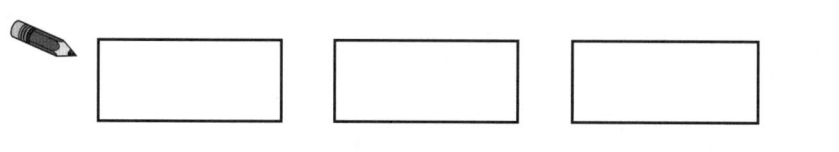

1 mark

Set A: Test 1

7. At a hockey match there are 480 people.
45% of people at the hockey match are wearing T-shirts.

How many people are **not** wearing T-shirts?

Show your working. You may get a mark.

2 marks

8. Pupils in Rosa's class record their favourite type of fish.
She puts the results on a pie chart.

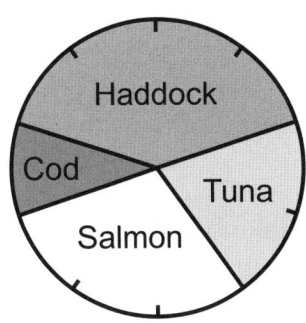

There are 40 pupils in Rosa's class.

How many pupils said salmon was their favourite?

1 mark

END OF TEST

/ 10

 **Bonus Brainteaser**

Look at the pie chart in Q8. If 8 pupils who chose haddock swapped their answer to tuna, what percentage of the pie chart would be covered by tuna?

Set A: Test 2

There are **8 questions** in this test. Give yourself **10 minutes** to answer them all.

1. Complete the calculations below.

   304.5 ÷ 100 = ☐

   3.045 × ☐ = 3045

   1 mark

2. Circle the factors of 52.

   1   3   13   19

   1 mark

3. Rosa is making a patchwork blanket.
   Each rectangular patch will measure 60 mm by 40 mm.

   Using a ruler and protractor, draw an accurate 60 mm by 40 mm rectangle.

   One side has been drawn for you.

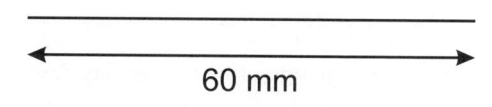

   60 mm

   1 mark

Set A: Test 2

4. On a roundabout at a playground there are 8 bars with equal angles between them, as shown below.

What is the size of each angle?

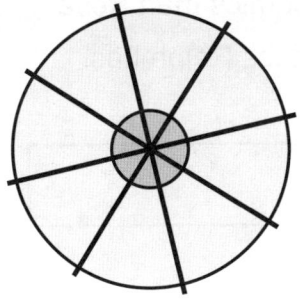

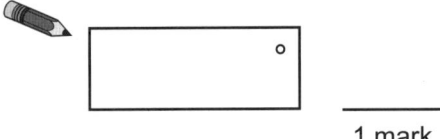

1 mark

5. Ozzy and Ralph played darts. For every 5 points that Ozzy scored, Ralph scored 7. The total number of points scored was 60.

How many points did Ralph score?

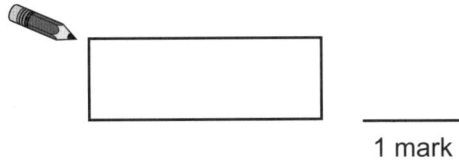

1 mark

6. Complete this calculation, giving your answer as a mixed number.

$$\frac{3}{8} + \frac{9}{10} = \boxed{}$$

1 mark

7. Ozzy, Rosa and Ralph are comparing their comic collections. The number of comics that Ozzy has is C. Rosa has 4 times as many comics as Ozzy. Ralph has 5 more comics than Rosa.

Write an expression that shows how many comics Ralph has.

1 mark

Ozzy has 12 comics. How many comics does Ralph have?

1 mark

8. Ralph is cutting a carpet to fit his hallway. A plan of his hallway is shown below.

Calculate the perimeter and area of his hallway.

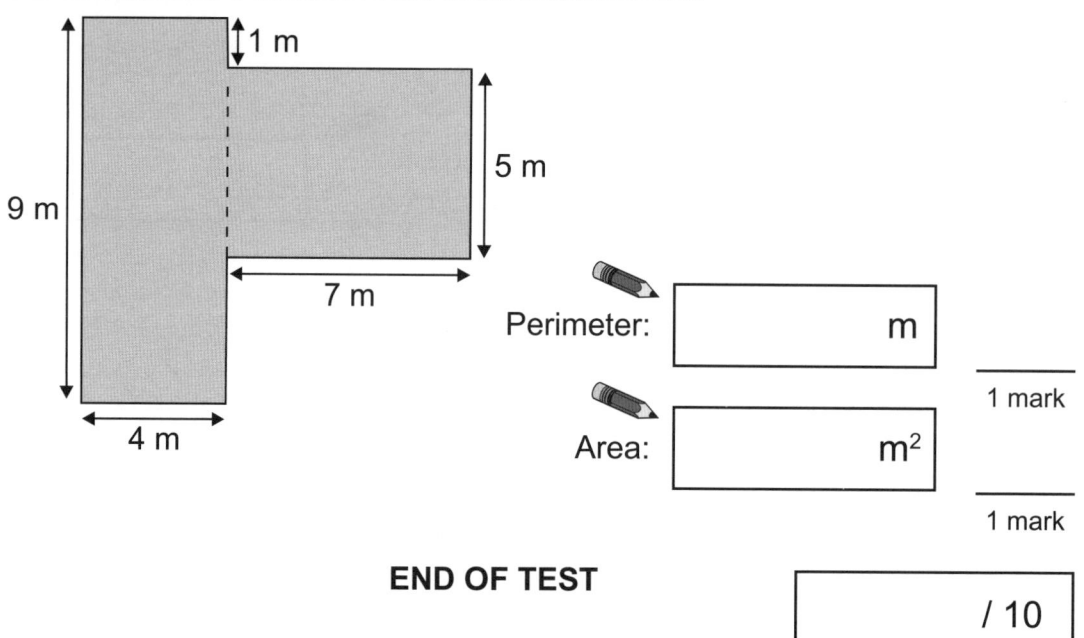

Perimeter: ___ m

1 mark

Area: ___ m²

1 mark

END OF TEST

/ 10

Bonus Brainteaser

In Q8, Ralph starts with an 8 m by 10 m rectangle of carpet. What is the minimum number of pieces Ralph will need to use to fully cover his hallway floor?

Set A: Test 3

There are **8 questions** in this test. Give yourself **10 minutes** to answer them all.

1. Join the numbers on the left to their value when rounded to **1 decimal place**.

   16.245   16.3

   16.31   16.2

   15.88   15.9

   1 mark

2. Rosa goes karting with friends. The karting track is 500 m long.

   If she goes around the track nine times, how many **kilometres** will she have travelled?

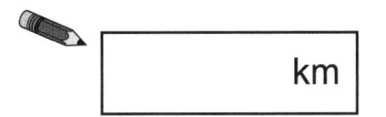

   ☐ km

   1 mark

3. Write down the two common multiples of 3 and 7 that are less than 50.

   ☐ and ☐

   1 mark

4. Rosa is posting a box. It costs £3.00 to post a box with a volume greater than 1500 cm³, otherwise it costs £2.00.

How much would it cost Rosa to post the box below?

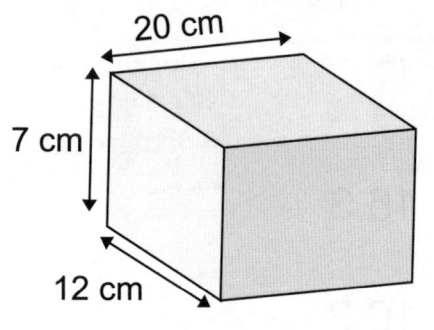

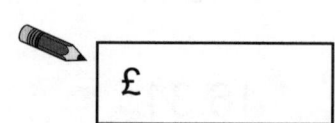

£

1 mark

5. Work out the size of angles x and y in the isosceles triangle below.

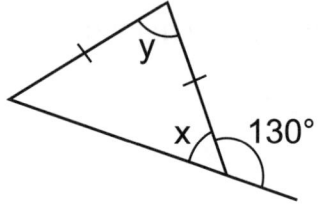

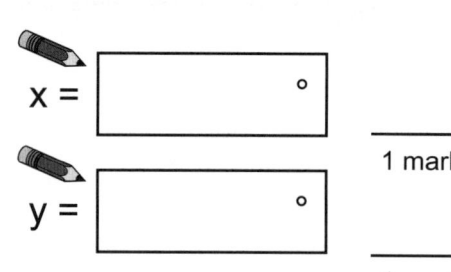

x = ___ °

1 mark

y = ___ °

1 mark

6. Fill in the missing number to make this fraction calculation correct.

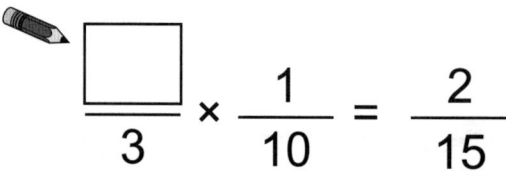

$$\frac{\Box}{3} \times \frac{1}{10} = \frac{2}{15}$$

1 mark

Set A: Test 3   8   © CGP — not to be photocopied

7. On a map 3 cm represents 75 m in real life. The distance between a hotel and the train station is 11 cm on the map.

What is the real life distance from the hotel to the train station?

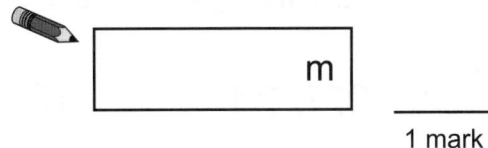 m

1 mark

8. In 2002, Ralph bought a rare video game for £40.
This year, he sold the video game for 75% more than he paid for it.

How much did he sell the video game for?

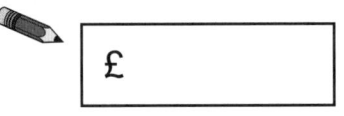 £

1 mark

Another video game that Ralph bought in 2002 for £22 is now only worth 52% of its original value.

How much is this game worth now?

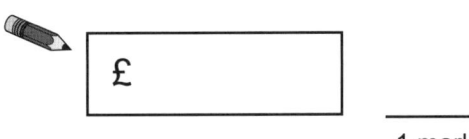 £

1 mark

END OF TEST   / 10

 **Bonus Brainteaser**

Rosa collects trading cards. 1 in 12 of her cards is a rare card. She gives away 2 rare cards and has 250 cards left. How many rare cards does she have left?

Set A: Test 4

There are **8 questions** in this test. Give yourself **10 minutes** to answer them all.

1. By estimating the value of 309.4 × 9.6, circle the correct answer.

   4026.24   1879.24   2970.24

   _____
   1 mark

2. Complete the long multiplication below.

   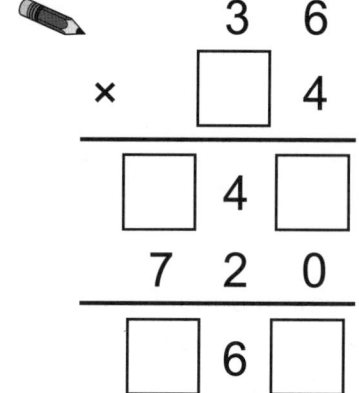

   _____
   1 mark

3. Fill in the missing number in the calculation below.

   $\frac{5}{8} \div \boxed{} = \frac{5}{24}$

   _____
   1 mark

Set A: Test 4   10   © CGP — not to be photocopied

4. Shape S is translated +4 units horizontally and –6 units vertically.

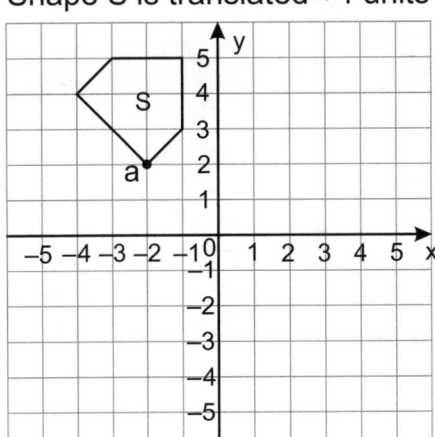

What are the coordinates of point a on the translated shape?

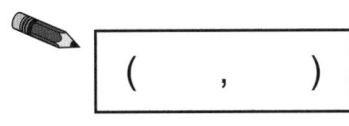

1 mark

5. The parallelogram below is enlarged by a scale factor of 7.

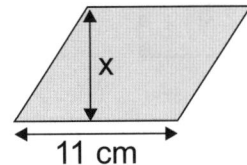

What is the base length of the enlarged parallelogram?

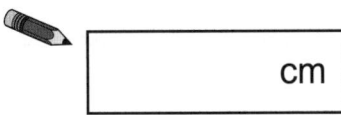 cm

1 mark

The enlarged parallelogram has a height of 630 mm.

What is the height, x, of the original parallelogram, in cm?

x = 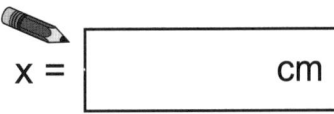 cm

1 mark

6. The number of days it takes to build a shed, D, is worked out using the formula: D = 7 + 3R – W, where R is the number of rainy days and W is the number of workers.

If there are 4 rainy days and 3 workers, how many days will it take to build the shed?

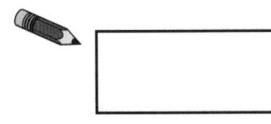

1 mark

7. Ralph owns red ties and blue ties. He has 36 ties in total.
He has 3 times as many blue ties as red ties.

How many **blue ties** does Ralph own?

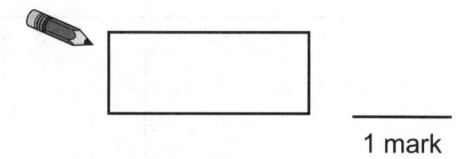

1 mark

8. Five people at a guitar shop are asked how many guitars they own.
The results are shown in the table below.

Name	Axel	Bonnie	Bruce	Ozzy	Brian
Number of guitars	6	1	3	?	5

The mean number of guitars is 4.

How many guitars does Ozzy own?

Show your working. You may get a mark.

2 marks

END OF TEST

/ 10

Bonus Brainteaser

A guitar has six strings. The first string has a thickness of $\frac{6}{5}$ mm.
The second string is $\frac{3}{4}$ as thick as the first string.
The third string is $\frac{3}{4}$ as thick as the second string.
What is the thickness of the third string?

Set A: Test 5

There are **8 questions** in this test. Give yourself **10 minutes** to answer them all.

1. 21 footballers each score the same number of goals in one season. The total number of goals scored is 483.

   How many goals did each footballer score?

   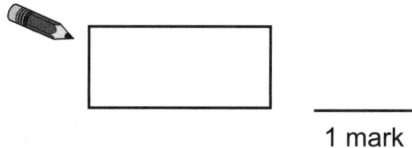

   1 mark

2. Place a <, > or = in the box to make the statement correct.

   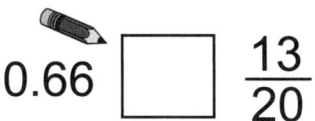

   1 mark

3. The sequence 1, 3, 9, 27... uses the rule "multiply by the same number each time".

   Write down the next two terms of the sequence.

   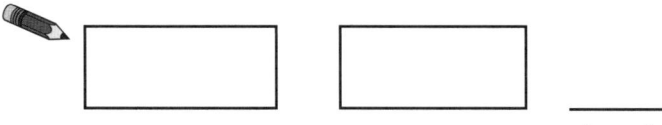

   1 mark

© CGP — not to be photocopied

4. Order the fractions below from **largest** to **smallest**.

$$\frac{5}{6} \quad \frac{1}{2} \quad \frac{1}{4} \quad \frac{4}{9}$$

Largest   Smallest

☐ ☐ ☐ ☐

1 mark

5. Ozzy is making a 3D shape out of card. He plans out what he wants his shape to look like on this diagram.

Draw a net of the shape on the grid below.

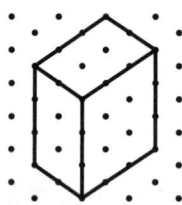

1 mark

6. Every weekend Ralph travels 44 km to visit his family.

Approximately how far is this in miles?

5 miles ≈ 8 km

miles

1 mark

Set A: Test 5   14   © CGP — not to be photocopied

7. Reflect shape K in the x-axis. Label the reflected shape L.

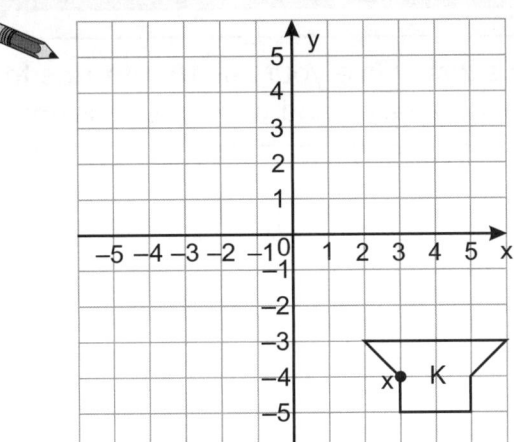

1 mark

Shape L is reflected in the y-axis to give shape M.

What are the coordinates of point x on shape M?

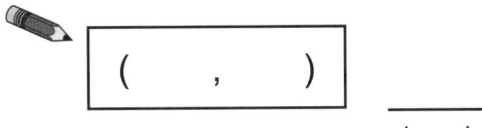

(,)

1 mark

8. Two cafes reduce the size of their drinks.
The drinks at cafe A decrease from 400 ml to 320 ml.
The drinks at cafe B decrease from 300 ml to 225 ml.

Which cafe reduces the size of its drinks by the **bigger percentage**?

Show your working. You may get a mark.

Cafe ☐

2 marks

END OF TEST

/ 10

?? Bonus Brainteaser

Ozzy's digital clock is missing some bits off the numbers.
Can you still work out what time it is from this digital display?

Set A: Arithmetic Test

There are **8 questions** in this test. Give yourself **10 minutes** to answer them all. Show your working in the spaces and write your answers in the boxes.

1. −129 + 900

   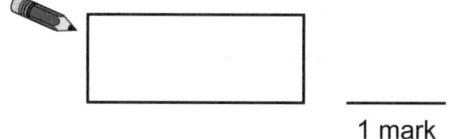

   1 mark

2. 24.5 − 9.36

   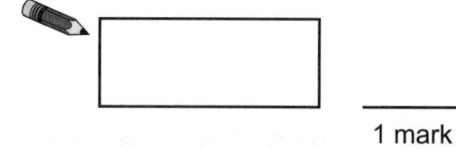

   1 mark

3. 48 − 20 × 2

   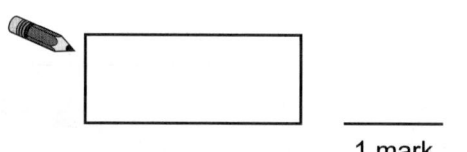

   1 mark

4. 1.35 × 8

   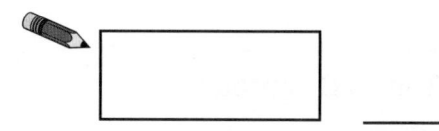

   1 mark

Set A: Arithmetic Test

5. $7^2 + 10$

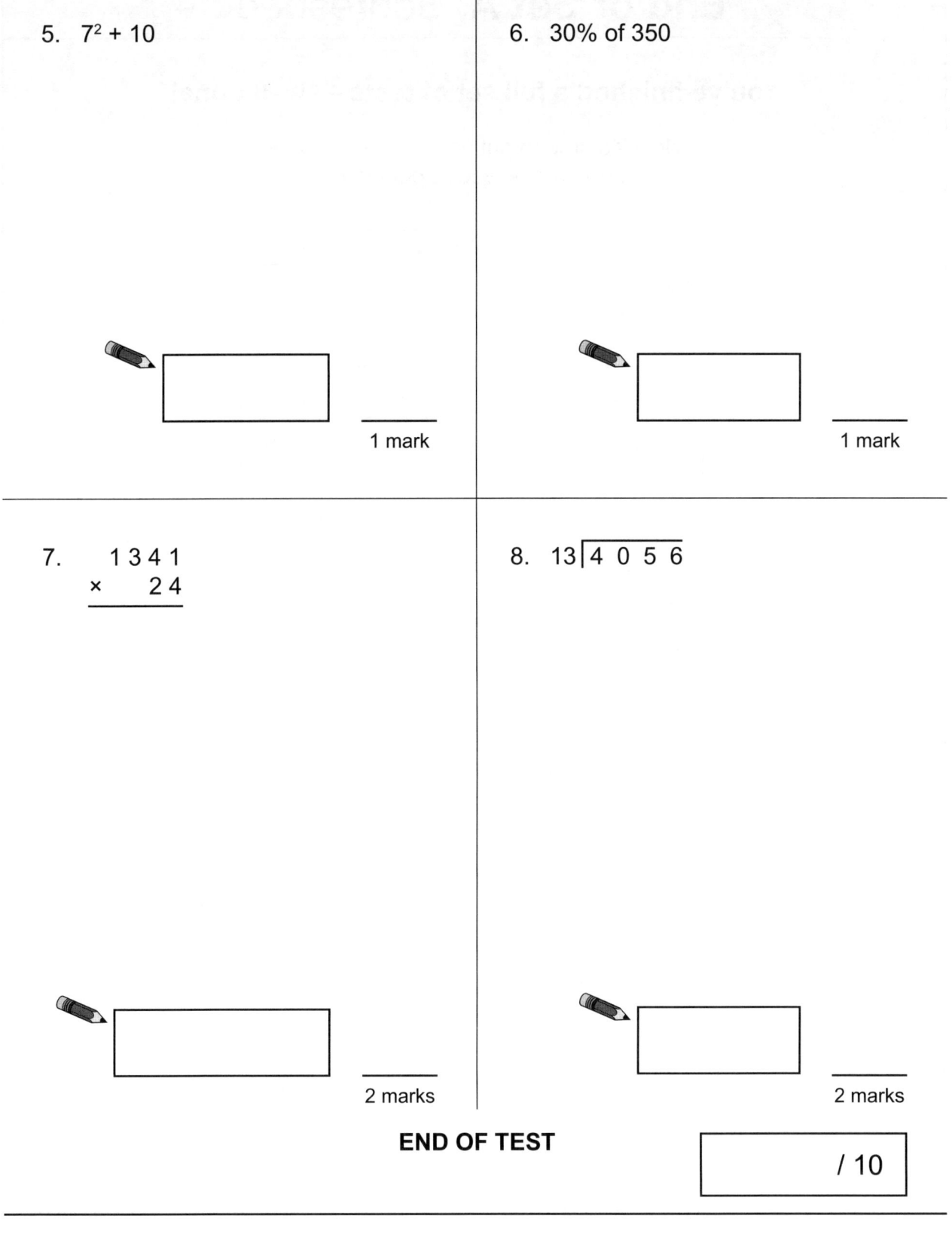

1 mark

6. 30% of 350

1 mark

7. $1\,3\,4\,1$
   $\times2\,4$

2 marks

8. $13\overline{)4\,0\,5\,6}$

2 marks

END OF TEST

/ 10

End of Set A: Scoresheet

You've finished a full set of tests — well done!

Now it's time to put your scores in here
and see how you're getting on.

	Score	
Test 1		/10
Test 2		/10
Test 3		/10
Test 4		/10
Test 5		/10
Arithmetic Test		/10
Total		**/60**

Once you've got a score out of 60, check it out in the table below...

0 – 29	If you got a lot of questions wrong, don't worry. **Practise** the topics you struggled with, then **have another go** at **this** set of tests.
30 – 45	If you got half-marks or better, you're doing well. Look back through the questions you got wrong and **brush up** on those topics. Then try the **next set** of tests.
46 – 60	Woohoo! Now have a go at the **next set** of tests — can you beat your score?

And did you solve all of the end-of-test teasers?

Set B: Test 1

There are **8 questions** in this test. Give yourself **10 minutes** to answer them all.

1. Fill in the missing number in this calculation.

    600 909 = 600 000 + ☐ + 9

    1 mark

2. Look at these temperatures: 9 °C, 13 °C, −2 °C, −4 °C, 5 °C.

    Find the **difference** between the highest and lowest temperatures.

    ☐ °C

    1 mark

3. The graph shows the conversion rate between rupees and euros.

    How much is 2 euros in rupees?

    ☐ rupees

    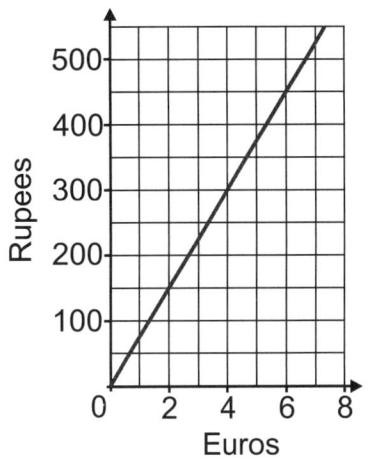

    1 mark

    Deeta gives 450 rupees worth of euros to her friend. How many euros is this?

    ☐ euros

    1 mark

4. For each of the following, choose the most sensible measurement from the box.

m³	kg
km	
	g	cm
ml	m

Mass of a scone ☐

Volume of a mug ☐

1 mark

5. Louise wants to enlarge the diagram of the room shown below by a scale factor of 2.

Draw the enlarged diagram on the grid below.

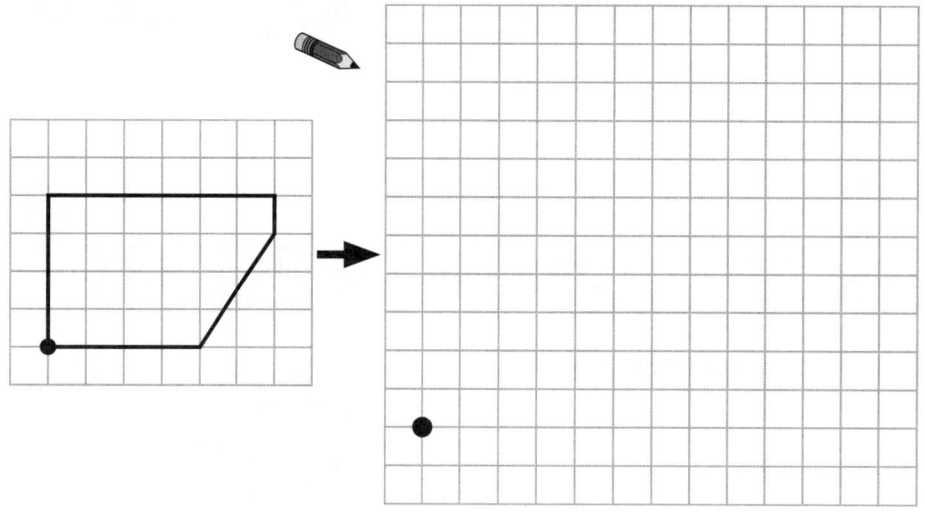

1 mark

6. Jaden and Louise recorded how many butterflies they each caught. For every 3 butterflies Jaden caught, Louise caught 4 butterflies.

Jaden caught 12 butterflies. How many butterflies did they catch in total?

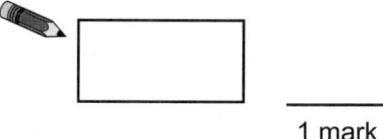

1 mark

Set B: Test 1   20   © CGP — not to be photocopied

7. Look at the diagram of the triangular prism below.

   Circle the net that matches the prism.

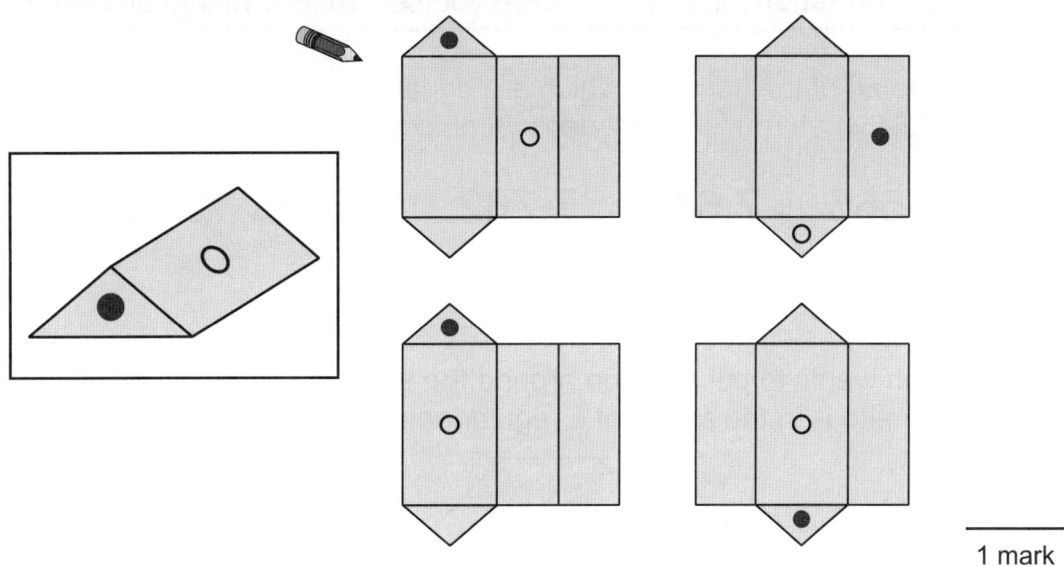

1 mark

8. Deeta wins 16 tokens at an arcade and trades them all for teddies and dolls. A teddy costs 3 tokens and a doll costs 2 tokens.

   Write down **all** the possible pairs of values for t and d, where t is the number of teddies and d is the number of dolls that she trades for.

2 marks

END OF TEST

/ 10

Bonus Brainteaser

5 bees enter an empty beehive at 3:00 am. From then on 11 bees enter and 3 bees leave the beehive each hour. How many bees are in the hive at 9:00 pm?

Set B: Test 2

There are **8 questions** in this test. Give yourself **10 minutes** to answer them all.

1. Circle **all** of the numbers which are equal to 7.64 when rounded to 2 decimal places.

   7.565   7.645   7.762   7.643   7.638

   _____
   1 mark

2. Jaden wants to put a ribbon around the edge of a cake. The cake is in the shape of a regular octagon.

   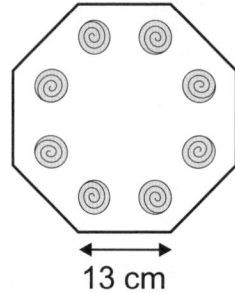
   13 cm

   What is the shortest length of ribbon needed for it to wrap **twice** around the cake?

   [ ] cm

   _____
   1 mark

3. Fill in the missing numbers to make these fractions equivalent.

   $\dfrac{9}{36} = \dfrac{3}{\boxed{}} = \dfrac{\boxed{}}{60}$

   _____
   1 mark

Set B: Test 2   22   © CGP — not to be photocopied

4. Every day Deeta takes 13 photographs.

How many photographs will she take in total during July and August?

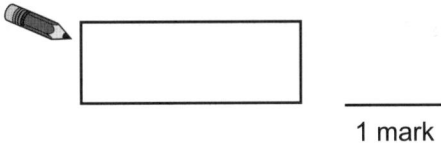

1 mark

5. Shape A is reflected so that the image of vertex m is (–5, 4).

Draw the reflection of Shape A on the grid.

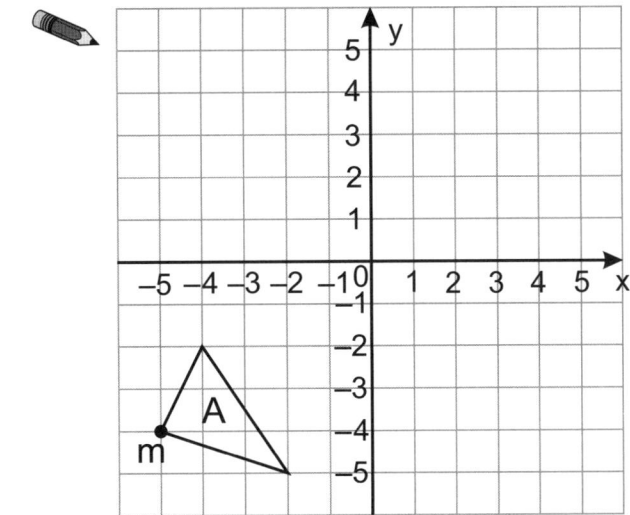

1 mark

6. Find the missing angle X.

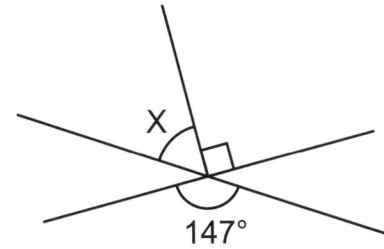

X = ☐ °

1 mark

7. On a farm, during one day, 1200 vegetables are picked.
   63% of the vegetables picked are carrots,
   26% are onions and 11% are parsnips.

   How many onions and carrots are picked in total on this day?

   Show your working. You may get a mark.

   2 marks

8. As part of an exercise routine Louise goes for a walk.
   After every 15 steps Louise does 5 star jumps.

   If Louise walks 240 steps, how many star jumps will she do?

   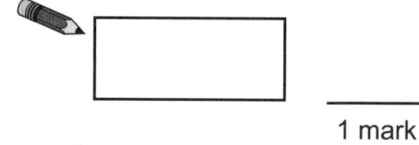

   1 mark

   Louise ends up doing 150 star jumps on her walk.

   How many steps did she do?

   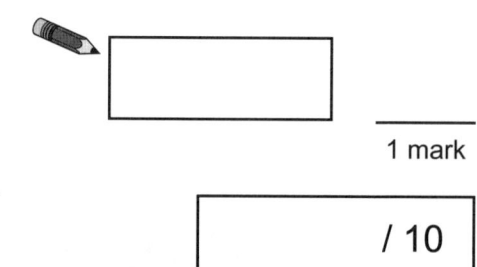

   1 mark

END OF TEST

/ 10

?? Bonus Brainteaser

Every time Louise walks 15 steps or does 5 star jumps she burns 1 calorie. She burnt 70 calories doing the same routine as in Q8. How many steps did she do?

Set B: Test 2

Set B: Test 3

There are **8 questions** in this test. Give yourself **10 minutes** to answer them all.

1. Louise pays £1.45 for a pack of sausages.
   How much will she pay for 6 packs of sausages?

   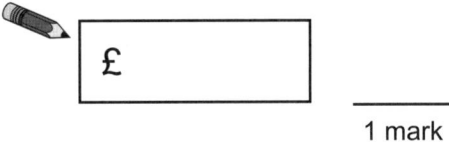

   1 mark

2. Find the highest common factor of 27 and 45.

   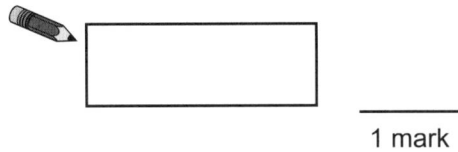

   1 mark

3. The weather is recorded in Perstone over the course of 40 days.
   It rains on 18 of the days. What is this as a percentage?

   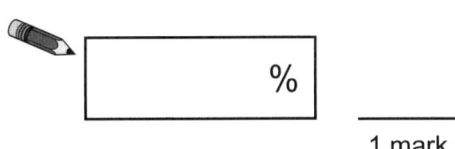

   1 mark

4. The first four numbers of a sequence are shown below.
The sequence uses the rule "multiply the previous term by 3 and add 2".

$$1 \quad\quad 5 \quad\quad 17 \quad\quad 53$$

Work out the **next term** of the sequence.

1 mark

5. Jaden is patching up a hole in his football. The patch will be a regular pentagon, with sides of 4 cm and interior angles of 108°.

Accurately draw Jaden's patch below using a ruler and protractor.

One side has been drawn for you.

2 marks

6. Triangle M has a point T at coordinates (1, 5).

If triangle M is translated +4 units horizontally and –8 units vertically, what will be the new coordinates of point T?

(,)

1 mark

Set B: Test 3   26   © CGP — not to be photocopied

7. Deeta only drinks squash that is 3 parts cordial and 11 parts water.

   If Deeta puts 154 ml of water in a glass, how much cordial should she use?

   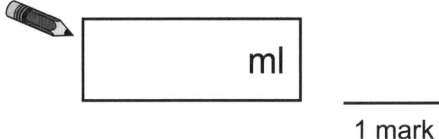

   ml

   1 mark

8. In a board game, players work out their score using this formula.

   $$\text{Score} = \frac{\text{Number on dice} + 14}{4}$$

   Jaden rolls a 6. What is his score for this roll?

   1 mark

   On her final turn Deeta needs a score of 4.5 or more to win.

   What is the **lowest** number Deeta could roll on the dice to win?

   1 mark

END OF TEST

/ 10

?? Bonus Brainteaser

A dog is chasing a cat. The cat runs 9 m every second and the dog runs 24 m every 2 seconds. The cat starts 27 m in front. How long will it take the dog to catch the cat?

Set B: Test 4

There are **8 questions** in this test. Give yourself **10 minutes** to answer them all.

1. Louise's cow eats 13 kg of food every day.
   How many days would it take for the cow to eat 299 kg of food?

   1 mark

2. Circle any shapes that have an area of 48 cm^2.

   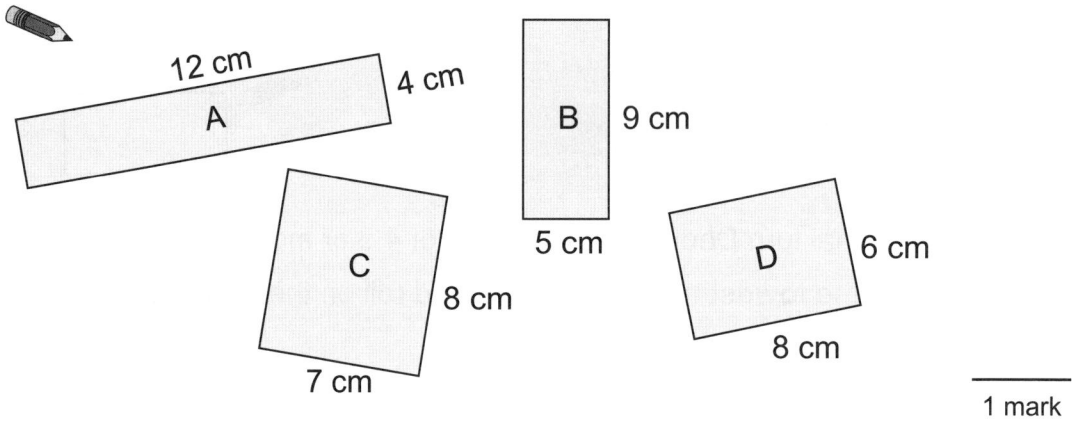

   1 mark

3. Circle the calculation which gives the same answer as 8 × 11 − 47

   4 × 12 − 5   98 − 7 × 7

   36 + 20 ÷ 4

   1 mark

Set B: Test 4   28   © CGP — not to be photocopied

4. Jaden is 64% of the way through his homework.

What fraction of his homework does he have left to do?

Give your answer in its simplest form.

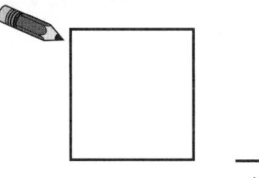

1 mark

5. A car salesman records how many cars he sells each week and plots the results on a bar chart.

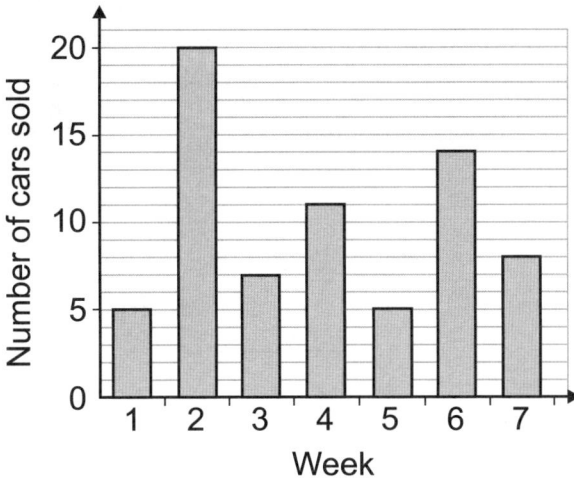

How many **more** cars were sold in week 6 than in week 7?

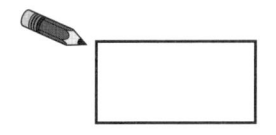

1 mark

What is the mean number of cars sold per week?

Show your working. You may get a mark.

2 marks

6. Deeta is making sandwiches for a party and starts with $2\frac{2}{3}$ loaves of bread. When she has finished, she has $\frac{5}{6}$ of a loaf left.

How many loaves of bread has she used?

1 mark

7. Jaden has two raffle tickets. Each ticket has a number on it. One number is 7 times greater than the other number. If he adds the two numbers together he gets 48.

What are the numbers on Jaden's tickets?

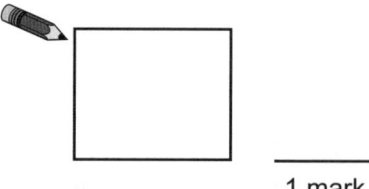

and

1 mark

8. Some of the vertices of a regular hexagon are labelled with coordinates.

Find the coordinates of point P.

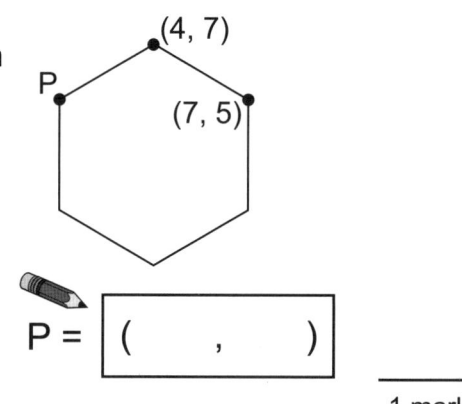

P = (,)

1 mark

END OF TEST

/ 10

?? Bonus Brainteaser

Louise has 3 raffle tickets from Q7. All of the numbers are prime numbers, they add up to 43 and the difference between the largest and smallest numbers is 16. What are her ticket numbers?

Set B: Test 5

There are **7 questions** in this test. Give yourself **10 minutes** to answer them all.

1. The distance from one side of a wheel to the other through the centre is 52 cm.

   What is the radius of the wheel?

   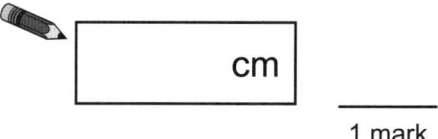

   1 mark

2. Fill in the missing digits to complete the calculation.

   $$\frac{4}{13} \times \frac{\square}{\square} = \frac{20}{39}$$

   1 mark

3. On Saturdays Deeta jogs from Lanchester to the lake, then from the lake to the forest.

   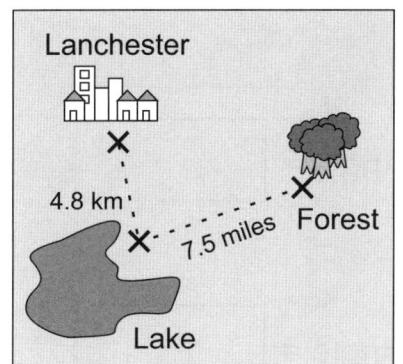

   How far does she jog in total? Give your answer in **kilometres**.

   5 miles ≈ 8 km

   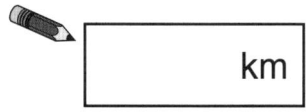

   1 mark

© CGP — not to be photocopied

Set B: Test 5

4. Use the operators (+, −, ×, ÷) to make this calculation correct.

7 ☐ 20 ☐ 4 = 12

1 mark

5. Louise says "For any prime number p, the expression 3p − 1 always gives an even answer."

Find an example to show that Louise is wrong.

1 mark

6. Work out the exterior and interior angles of a regular decagon.

Exterior Angle = ☐ °

1 mark

Interior Angle = ☐ °

1 mark

7. In a game, each colour of token is worth a different number of points (B, G and W). A full set of tokens is shown below.

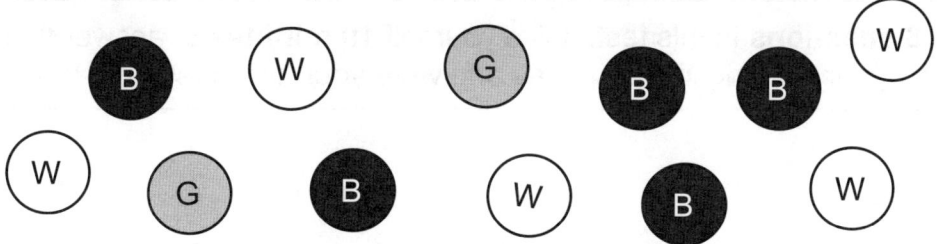

Write an expression using B, G and W to show the total number of points in a full set of tokens.

[ ]

1 mark

The full set of tokens is worth 71 points in total, and the black tokens are worth 12 points each. Each colour of token is worth a whole number of points.

Work out the value of the grey and white tokens.

Grey: [ ]   White: [ ]

2 marks

END OF TEST

/ 10

?? Bonus Brainteaser

Another game can be played with the set of tokens in Q7. In this game, the full set is only worth 22 points in total. B, G and W are all **positive whole numbers**. Find all the possible combinations of B, G and W.

Set B: Arithmetic Test

There are **8 questions** in this test. Give yourself **10 minutes** to answer them all. Show your working in the spaces and write your answers in the boxes.

1. 451 + 6872

   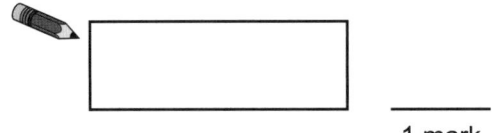

   1 mark

2. 23.1 × 9

   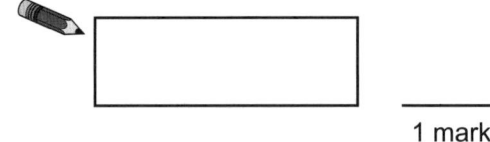

   1 mark

3. $\frac{2}{5} \div 4$

   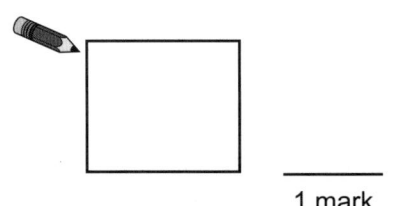

   1 mark

4. 120 × 12 ÷ 4

   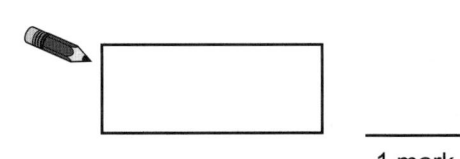

   1 mark

Set B: Arithmetic Test

5. $4\tfrac{1}{3} + 2\tfrac{5}{6}$

1 mark

6. 4% of 520

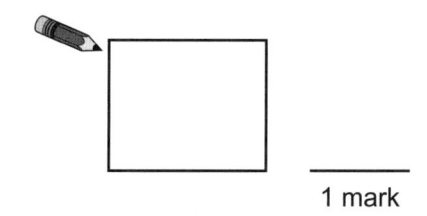

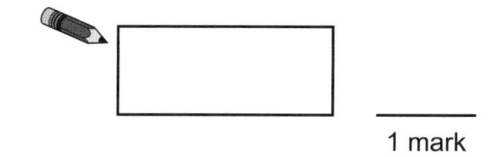

1 mark

7. $\begin{array}{r} 1226 \\ \times\quad 47 \\ \hline \end{array}$

2 marks

8. $19\overline{)5985}$

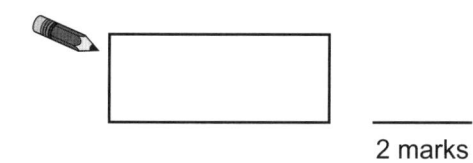

2 marks

END OF TEST

/ 10

End of Set B: Scoresheet

You've finished a full set of tests — well done!

Now it's time to put your scores in here
and see how you're getting on.

	Score	
Test 1		/10
Test 2		/10
Test 3		/10
Test 4		/10
Test 5		/10
Arithmetic Test		/10
Total		**/60**

Once you've got a score out of 60, check it out in the table below...

0 – 29	If you got a lot of questions wrong, don't worry. **Practise** the topics you struggled with, then **have another go** at **this** set of tests.
30 – 45	If you got half-marks or better, you're doing well. Look back through the questions you got wrong and **brush up** on those topics. Then try the **next set** of tests.
46 – 60	Woohoo! Now have a go at the **next set** of tests — can you beat your score?

And did you solve all of the end-of-test teasers?

Set B: Scoresheet

Set C: Test 1

There are **8 questions** in this test. Give yourself **10 minutes** to answer them all.

1. Fill in the missing digits to make this division correct.

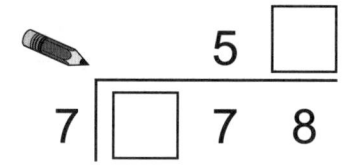

   $\;\;5\;\square$
   $7\,|\,\square\;7\;8$

   1 mark

2. Look at these number cards.

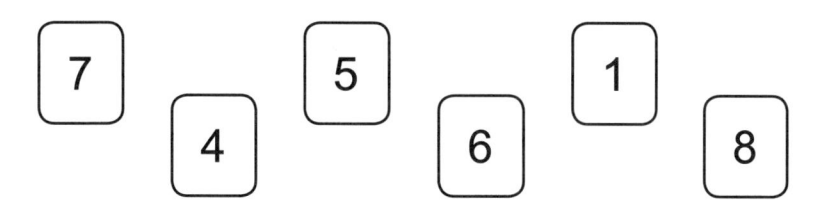

   | 7 | 5 | 1 |
   | 4 | 6 | 8 |

   Write down the **smallest odd number** you can make using **all** of the cards.

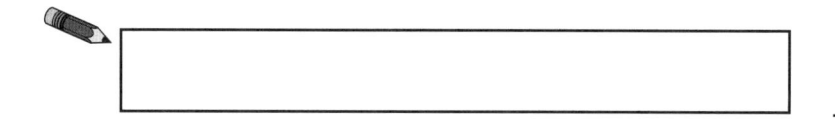

   1 mark

3. The shape below is made up of a square and triangle. Find the area of the shape.

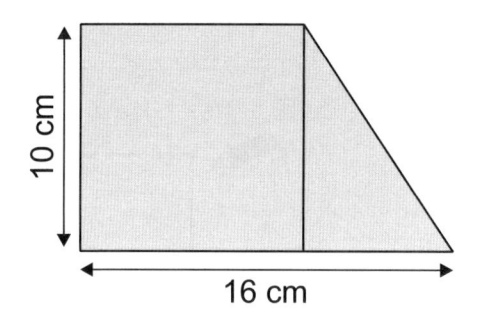

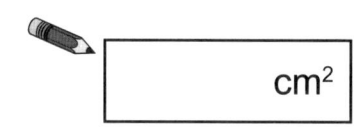

   10 cm
   16 cm

   ☐ cm²

   1 mark

© CGP — not to be photocopied

4. Find the size of angle X in the diagram below.

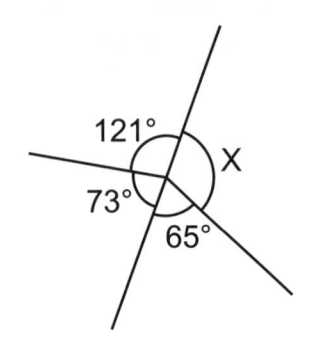

X = ☐°

1 mark

5. Given that 1000 ÷ 8 = 125, convert $\frac{1}{8}$ into a decimal.

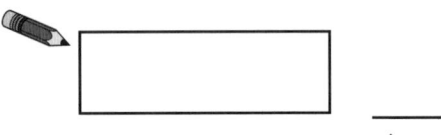

1 mark

6. Mei has two identical containers of water.
The first container is $\frac{3}{4}$ full, the second container is $\frac{1}{7}$ full.
She pours all the water from the second container into the first.

How full will the first container be now?

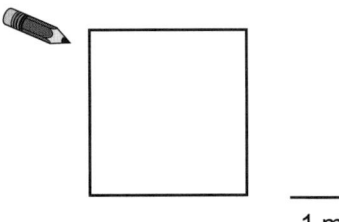

1 mark

Set C: Test 1

7. 72 adults are asked what their favourite place to stay on holiday is. The results are shown in the pie chart below.

Complete the table to show how many adults chose each option.

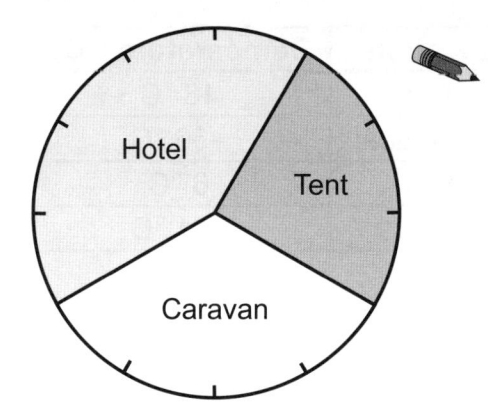

Favourite place to stay	Number of adults
Caravan	
Hotel	
Tent	

2 marks

8. Scott has a rectangular photo with a length of 15 cm and a width of 10 cm. He stretches the photo so its length is an enlargement of scale factor 5, and its width is an enlargement of scale factor 3.

What is the **area** of the enlarged photo?

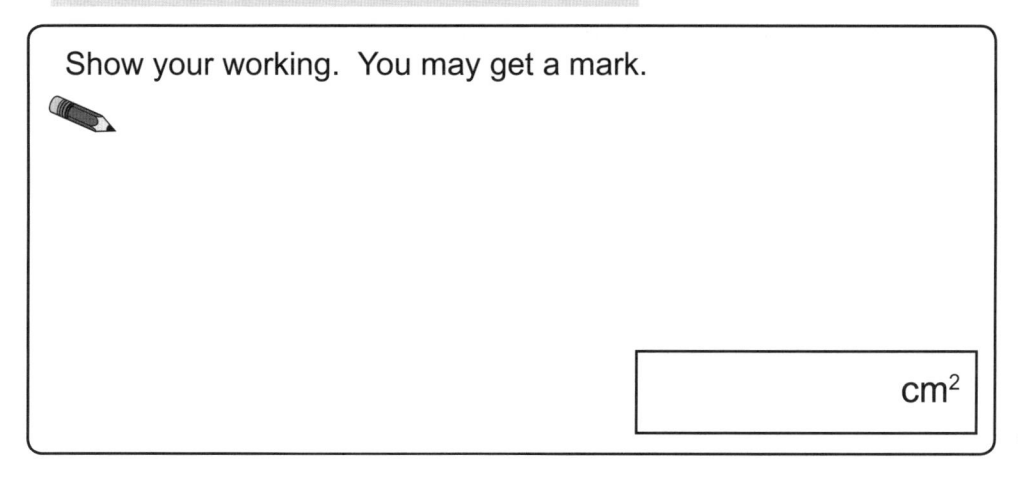

Show your working. You may get a mark.

cm^2

2 marks

END OF TEST

/ 10

Bonus Brainteaser

Using the number cards from Q2, how many two-digit prime numbers can you make? Are there any two-digit cube numbers you can make?

Set C: Test 2

There are **8 questions** in this test. Give yourself **10 minutes** to answer them all.

1. The temperatures in different locations were recorded at the start of March and put in the table on the right.

Location	Temperature (°C)
Iran	18 °C
Antarctica	−56 °C
Italy	6 °C
Canada	−11 °C

What was the **difference** between the temperatures in Iran and Canada?

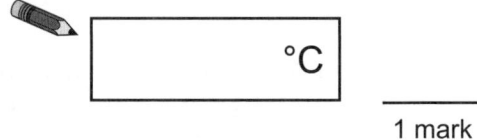

☐ °C

1 mark

At the end of March, the temperature in Antarctica was −89 °C.

What was the **difference** between the temperature in Antarctica at the start and end of March?

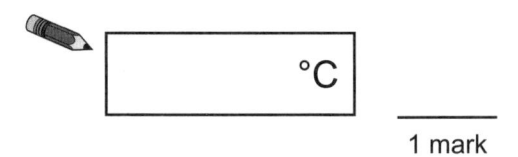

☐ °C

1 mark

2. To get home from school Morag cycles 1.4 km, gets a train for 6.8 km, and then cycles another 1.3 km.

How far does she travel in total?

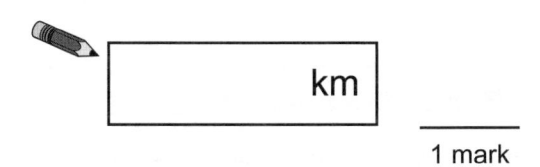

☐ km

1 mark

Set C: Test 2

3. Mei has two rolls of tape. The first roll has a diameter of 12 cm. The diameter of the second roll is half that of the first.

What is the **radius** of the second roll of tape?

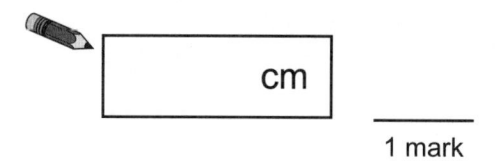

cm

1 mark

4. At a bakery, there are three times as many giant cookies (g) as small cookies (s) for sale.

Which of these equations is true? Circle the correct answer.

$3s = g$ $3 + g = s$ $g - 3 = s$ $3g = s$

1 mark

5. A square with a side length of 7 units is drawn on the set of axes below.

What are the coordinates of point P?

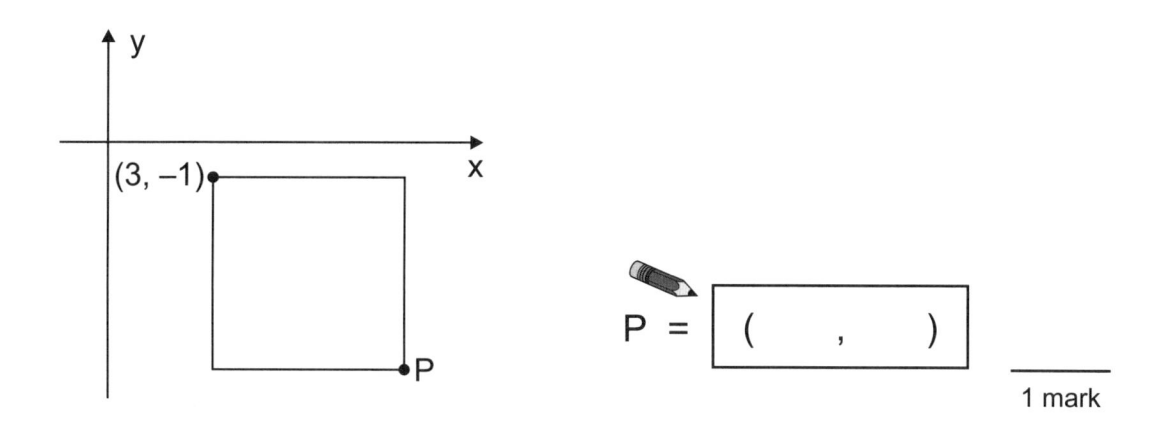

(3, −1)

P = (,)

1 mark

6. In January, Scott's band sell 160 albums.
   In February they sell 15% more albums than in January.

   How many albums do Scott's band sell in February?

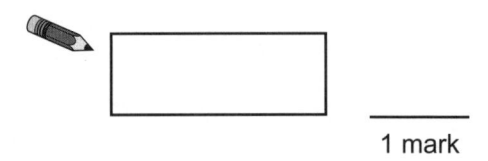

   [ ]

   1 mark

7. The weights of 6 onions are recorded and shown on the right.

   | 125 g | 100 g | 130 g |
   | 120 g | 90 g | 95 g |

   Circle the mean weight of the onions.

   115 g   132 g   110 g   120 g

   1 mark

8. A lawnmower's fuel tank contains $2\frac{1}{4}$ gallons of petrol.
   $1\frac{7}{12}$ gallons are used and then $\frac{2}{3}$ gallons are added.

   How many gallons of petrol are now in the lawnmower?

   Show your working. You may get a mark.

   [ ] gallons

   2 marks

END OF TEST

/ 10

?? Bonus Brainteaser

Two more onions (weighing the same amount) are added to the 6 onions in Q7.
The mean dropped to 105 g. Work out how much each extra onion weighed.

Set C: Test 2

Set C: Test 3

There are **8 questions** in this test. Give yourself **10 minutes** to answer them all.

1. Scott is filling a paper bag with eggs. The bag can hold a maximum of 0.5 kg, and each egg weighs 60 g.

   What is the maximum number of eggs Scott could put in the paper bag?

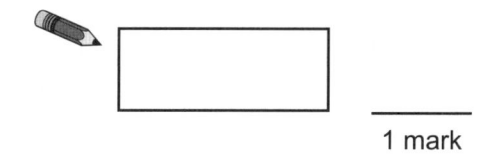

   1 mark

2. Complete the sequence by filling in the missing numbers.

   –4   –1   ☐   5   8   ☐   14

   1 mark

3. Triangle numbers are made by starting at 1 and adding each whole number in turn, e.g. 1 + 2 + 3 + 4 = 10, so 10 is a triangle number.

   Morag says, "28 is a triangle number". Show that she is correct.

   1 mark

4. In a multi-pack of crisps there are three flavours.
There are 11 packets of ready salted,
6 packets of roast chicken and 7 packets of BBQ.

What **percentage** of the packets are roast chicken flavour?

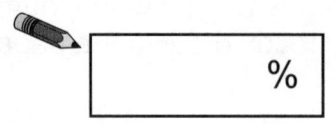

%

1 mark

5. Look at the equation below.

$$3a + b = 11$$

Find **all** the possible pairs of positive whole-number values for a and b.

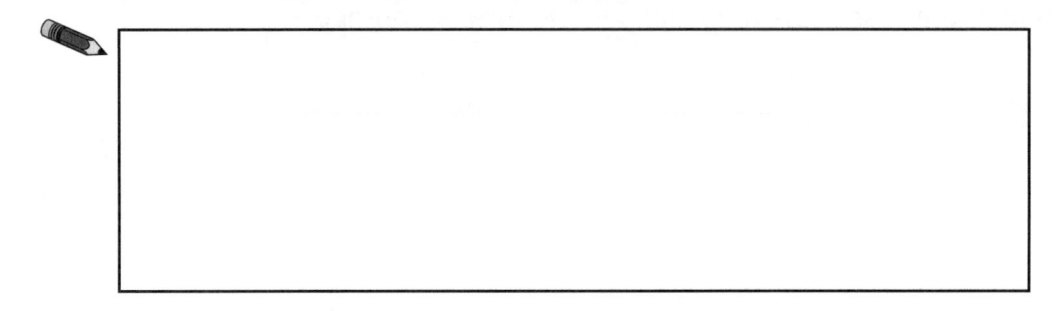

2 marks

6. Mei folds up the net below to make a cube.

Circle the cube which could be made from her net.

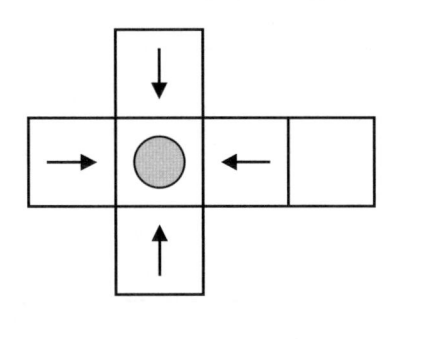

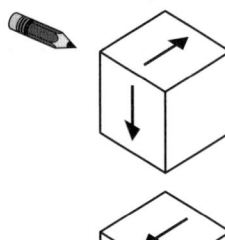

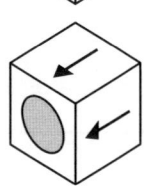

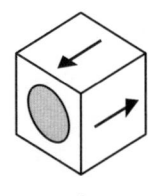

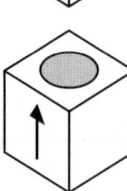

1 mark

Set C: Test 3

7. A regular nonagon has 9 sides of equal length. It has exterior angles of 40°.

Calculate the sum of **interior** angles of a regular nonagon.

☐ °

1 mark

8. In an orchard 3 types of apple grow. For every 4 red apples that grow, 2 green apples and 3 yellow apples grow.

If 56 red and yellow apples grow in total, how many green apples grow?

Show your working. You may get a mark.

2 marks

END OF TEST

/ 10

? Bonus Brainteaser

Mei makes a net of a cube. When folded, it can be rotated to look like **any** of the 4 cubes from Q6. Draw a possible net that Mei could have made.

Set C: Test 4

There are **8 questions** in this test. Give yourself **10 minutes** to answer them all.

1. There are 40 potatoes in a sack.
   Each potato weighs 0.16 kg and the sack weighs 0.4 kg.

   What is the total weight of a sack of potatoes?

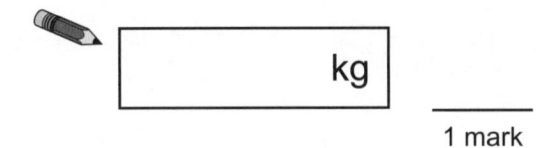

   ☐ kg

   1 mark

2. Complete the calculation by filling in the missing number.

   $9 \times \boxed{} - 31 = -4$

   1 mark

3. Morag works out that (20.134 + 29.878) × 7.101 = 206.132.
   Use estimation to show that her answer is **incorrect**.

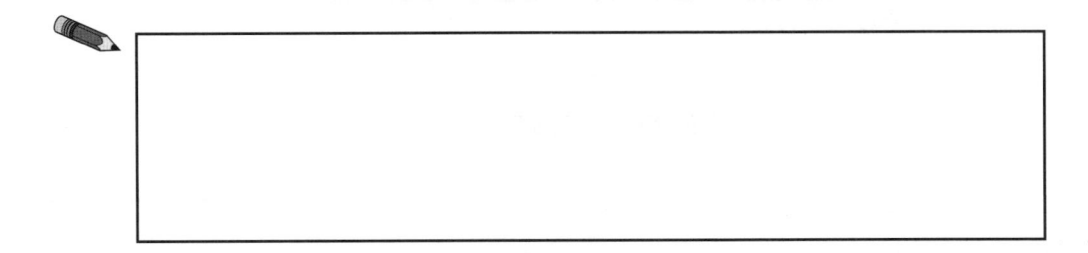

   1 mark

4. Scott makes this pattern using full bricks and half bricks.
What is the perimeter of his pattern?

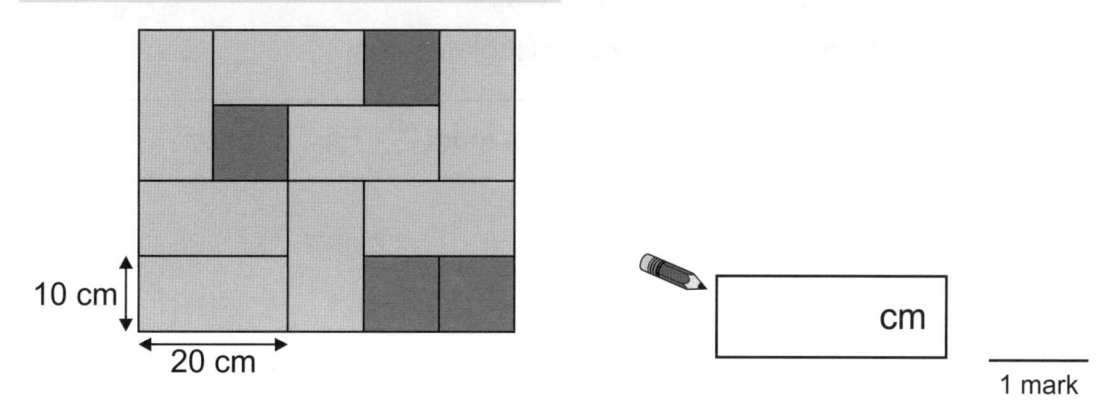

10 cm
20 cm

cm

1 mark

5. Morag buys a 1300 g bag of seed for the birds in her garden.
She puts 21% of the seed in the bird feeders.

How much seed has she used in the feeders?

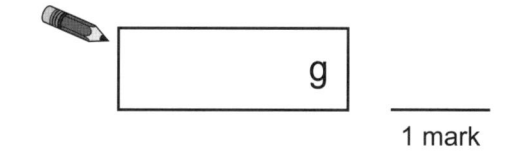

g

1 mark

6. A large cuboid stone trough is shown below.
The hole in the trough has a volume of 12.36 m³.

Calculate the volume of the stone that makes up the trough.

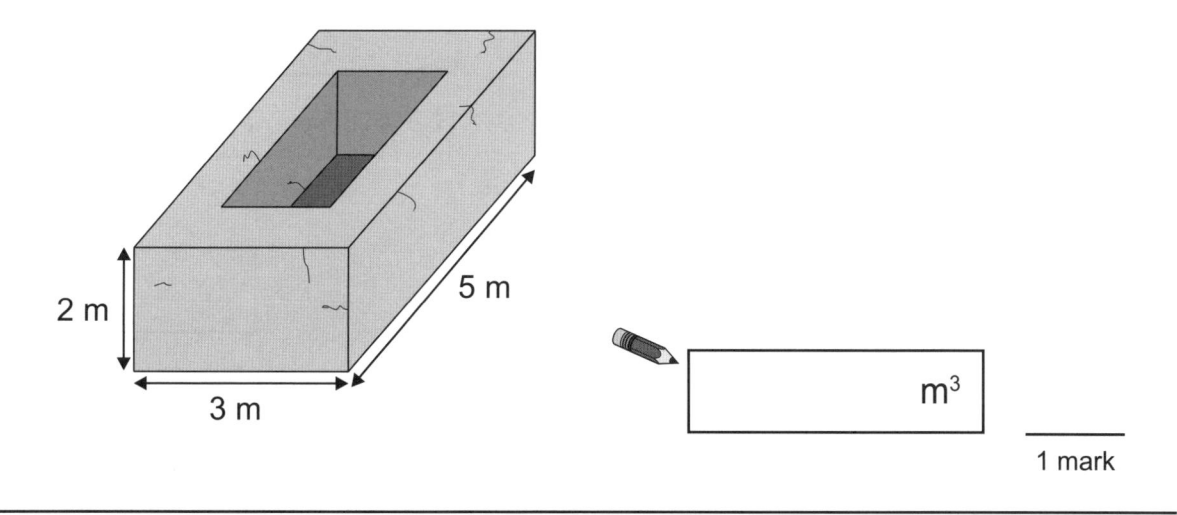

2 m
5 m
3 m

m³

1 mark

7. Mei buys a box of chocolates for £2.34. Her box contains 18 chocolates. Scott pays the same amount per chocolate and his box contains 23 chocolates.

   How much does Scott's box of chocolates cost?

   Show your working. You may get a mark.

   £ _____

   2 marks

8. Three identical triangles are drawn on the axes below.

   What are the coordinates of point R?

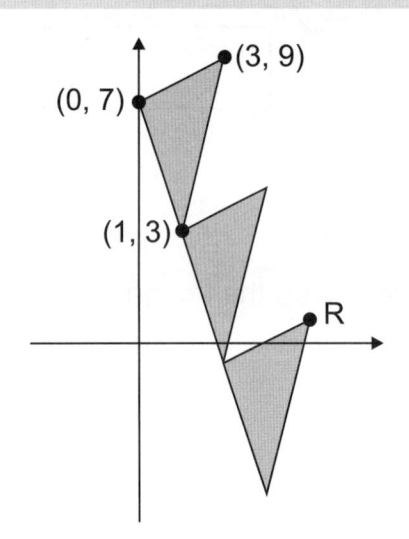

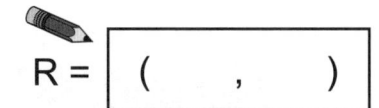

   (0, 7)
   (3, 9)
   (1, 3)
   R

   R = (,)

   2 marks

END OF TEST

/ 10

? Bonus Brainteaser

Mei has 2 yellow dresses, 1 red dress and 1 blue dress. How many different ways can she hang them up so that the yellow dresses do not hang next to each other?

Set C: Test 4

Set C: Test 5

There are **7 questions** in this test. Give yourself **10 minutes** to answer them all.

1. Draw three lines joining each fraction below to an equivalent fraction.

    $\frac{7}{6}$ $\frac{11}{12}$ $\frac{42}{36}$

    $\frac{48}{36}$ $\frac{33}{36}$ $\frac{8}{6}$

    _____
    1 mark

2. Write down three prime numbers which give 154 when multiplied together.

    [____] , [____] and [____]

    _____
    1 mark

3. Work out the size of angle a on the diagram below.

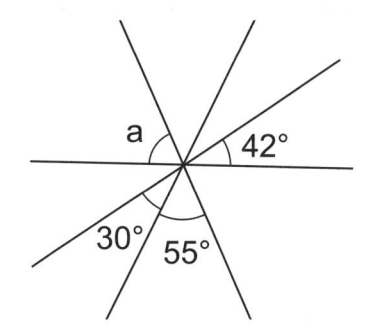

    a, 42°, 30°, 55°

    a = [____]°

    _____
    1 mark

© CGP — not to be photocopied

Set C: Test 5

4. Mei finds a recipe to make jam. To make 400 g of jam she needs 180 g of raspberries, 180 g of sugar and 40 g of grated lemon.

    How much sugar would Mei use to make 1 kg of jam?

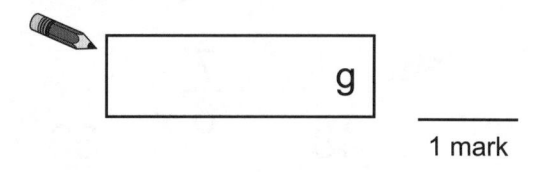

    [   ] g

    1 mark

    If Mei uses 50 g of grated lemon.

    How many grams of raspberries should she use?

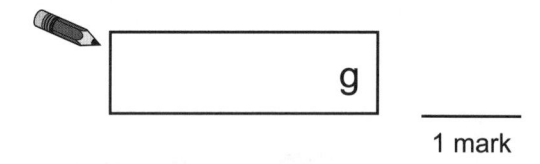

    [   ] g

    1 mark

5. Morag's suitcase weighs 20.219 kg.
    She takes out 3.675 kg of clothes and puts in 4.234 kg of gifts.

    By rounding each number to **1 decimal place**, estimate the weight of her suitcase after removing the clothes and adding the gifts.

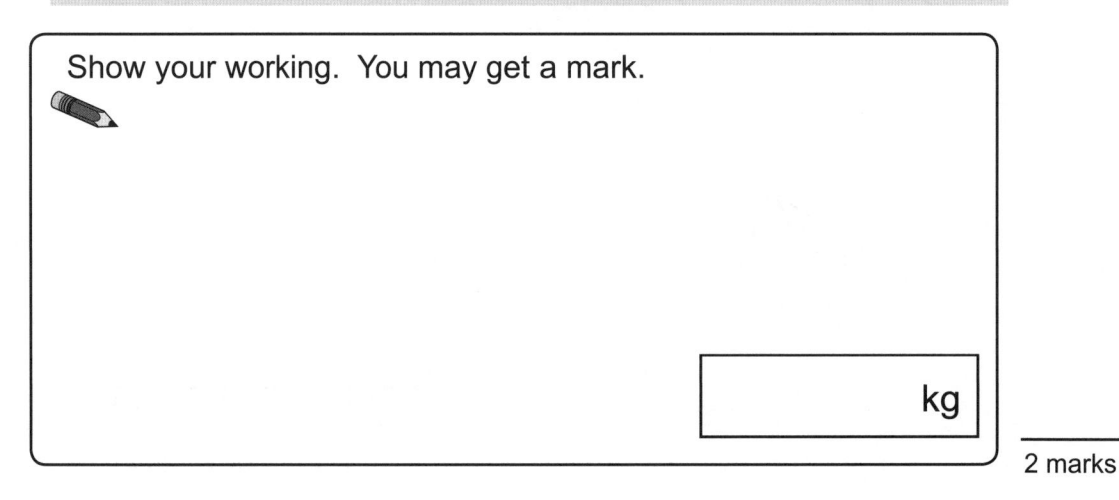

    Show your working. You may get a mark.

    [   ] kg

    2 marks

6. Scott places a counter on a coordinate grid at the coordinates (x, y) = (4, 6). The counter is moved such that its new coordinates are (2x + 1, 4 – 3y)

Write down the coordinates of the moved counter.

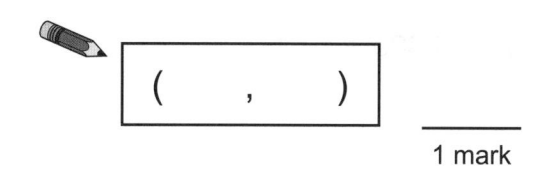

(,)

1 mark

7. Morag cuts out a kite shape from a rectangular piece of card as shown in this diagram.

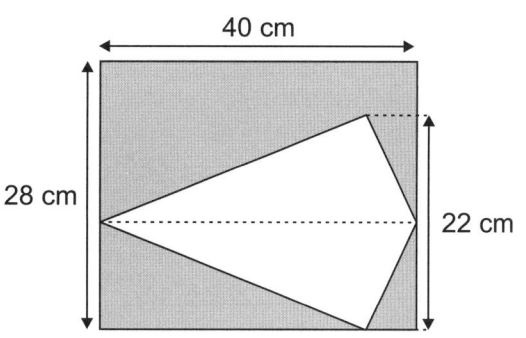

40 cm

28 cm

22 cm

What is the **shaded area** of the card?

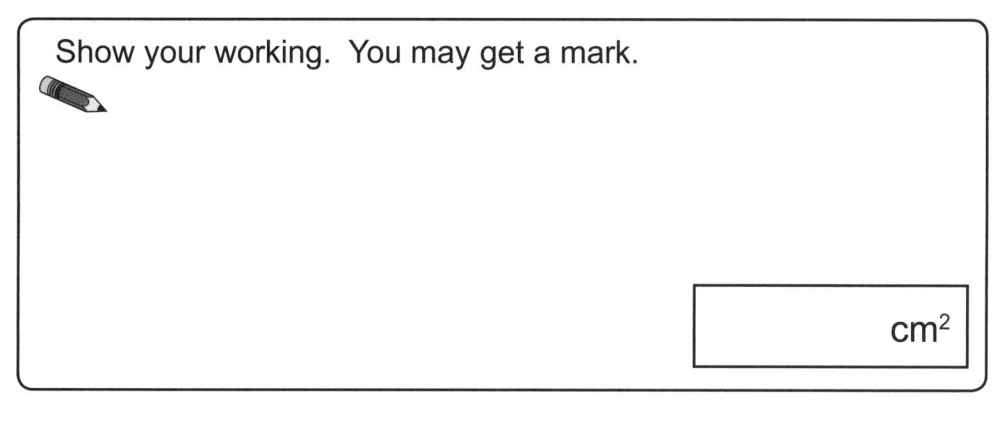

Show your working. You may get a mark.

cm²

2 marks

END OF TEST

/ 10

? Bonus Brainteaser

In Q6, Scott places a small black counter and large white counter centred on (0, 0). The black counter has a **diameter** of 1 unit. The edge of the white counter touches (2, 0). What is the scale factor of enlargement from the black counter to the white counter?

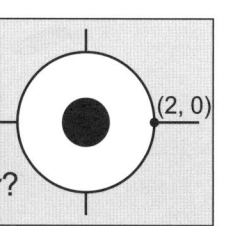

(2, 0)

© CGP — not to be photocopied   51   Set C: Test 5

Set C: Arithmetic Test

There are **8 questions** in this test. Give yourself **10 minutes** to answer them all. Show your working in the spaces and write your answers in the boxes.

1. 70 303 ÷ 1000

   1 mark

2. $\dfrac{3}{8} \div 6$

   1 mark

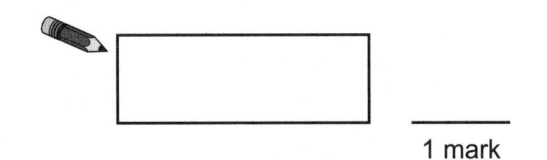

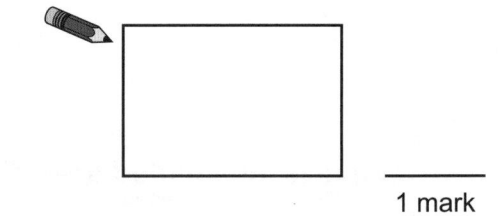

3. $6^2 + (7 - 2)^2$

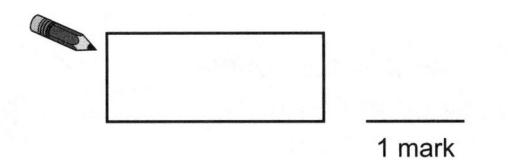

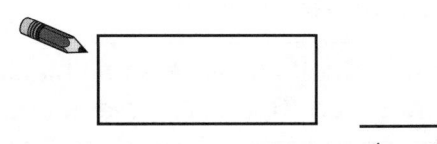

   1 mark

4. 37% of 800

   1 mark

Set C: Arithmetic Test

5. $3\frac{1}{7} - \frac{2}{3}$

1 mark

6. $24 \times 2\frac{1}{3}$

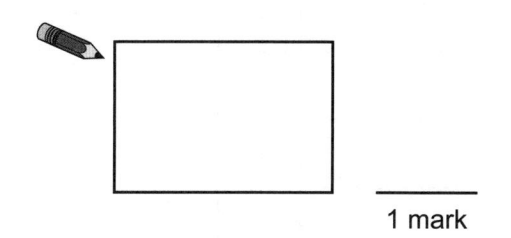

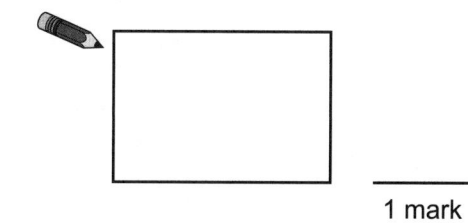

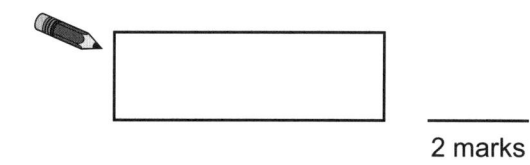

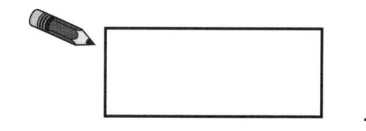

1 mark

7. $\quad\begin{array}{r}4526\\ \times\quad 39\\ \hline\end{array}$

2 marks

8. $27\overline{)8964}$

2 marks

END OF TEST

/ 10

End of Set C: Scoresheet

You've finished a full set of tests — well done!

Now it's time to put your scores in here
and see how you're getting on.

	Score	
Test 1		/10
Test 2		/10
Test 3		/10
Test 4		/10
Test 5		/10
Arithmetic Test		/10
Total		**/60**

Once you've got a score out of 60, check it out in the table below...

0 – 29	If you got a lot of questions wrong, don't worry. **Practise** the topics you struggled with, then **have another go** at **this** set of tests.
30 – 45	If you got half-marks or better, you're doing well. Look back through the questions you got wrong and **brush up** on those topics until you're happy with them.
46 – 60	Woohoo! You've done really well — congratulations.

And did you solve all of the end-of-test teasers?

Set C: Scoresheet

Answers

Set A

Test 1 — pages 1-3

1. **1 mark for both correct**
   378 746 to the nearest hundred is 378 700
   378 746 to the nearest thousand is 379 000

2. **1 mark**
   $40 - 6 \times 5 = 10$

3. **1 mark for correct answer**
   Area of triangle = $\frac{1}{2} \times 11 \times 8 = 44$ mm²

4. **1 mark for both correct**
   $\frac{9}{12}$ and 0.75

5. **1 mark for correct answer**
   1 pot of jam weighs $120 \div 2 = 60$ g
   5 pots of jam weigh $60 \times 5 = 300$ g

6. **1 mark**
   Add 2.5 each time
   1 mark for all correct
   12.5, 15, 17.5

7. **2 marks for correct answer**
   otherwise **1 mark for correct working**
   $100\% - 45\% = 55\%$ of people not wearing T-shirts
   50% of 480 = $480 \div 2 = 240$
   10% of 480 = 48, 5% of 480 = $48 \div 2 = 24$
   55% of 480 = 50% + 5% = $240 + 24 = 264$

8. **1 mark for correct answer**
   The pie chart is split into 10 equal sectors. There are 40 pupils in the class, so each sector is worth $40 \div 10 = 4$ pupils. Salmon takes up 3 sectors so $3 \times 4 = 12$ pupils said salmon was their favourite.

BONUS BRAINTEASER
Each sector is worth 4 pupils, so tuna gets bigger by $8 \div 4 = 2$ sectors and takes up $2 + 2 = 4$ sectors. This is $\frac{4}{10} = 40\%$ of the pie chart.

Test 2 — pages 4-6

1. **1 mark for both correct**
   $304.5 \div 100 = 3.045$
   $3.045 \times 1000 = 3045$

2. **1 mark for both correct**
   1 and 13

3. **1 mark for an accurately drawn rectangle**
   (40 mm by 60 mm)

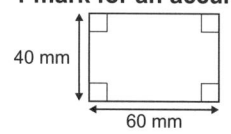

4. **1 mark for correct answer**
   Angles round a point = 360°
   $360° \div 8 = 45°$

5. **1 mark for correct answer**
   For every 5 points Ozzy scored, Ralph scored 7.
   There are $5 + 7 = 12$ shares in total.
   1 share = $60 \div 12 = 5$ points
   Ralph gets 7 shares = $7 \times 5 = 35$ points

6. **1 mark for correct answer**
   $\frac{3}{8} + \frac{9}{10} = \frac{15}{40} + \frac{36}{40} = \frac{51}{40} = 1\frac{11}{40}$

7. **1 mark**
   $4C + 5$
   1 mark for correct answer
   $4 \times 12 + 5 = 48 + 5 = 53$

8. **1 mark for correct answer**
   Fill in the missing sides: 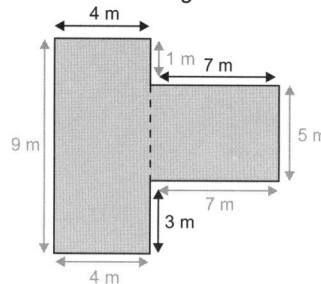

   Perimeter = $9 + 4 + 1 + 7 + 5 + 7 + 3 + 4 = 40$ m
   1 mark for correct answer
   Area = $(9 \times 4) + (7 \times 5) = 36 + 35 = 71$ m²

BONUS BRAINTEASER
He would need at least 3 pieces of carpet.
E.g. If he cut the carpet up as shown on the left and repositioned the pieces as shown on the right:

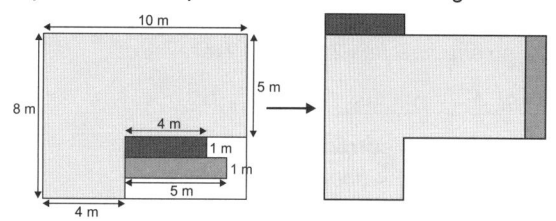

Test 3 — pages 7-9

1. **1 mark for all lines correct**
   16.245 — 16.3
   16.31 — 16.2
   15.88 — 15.9

55

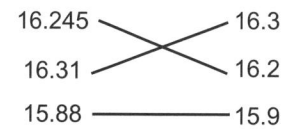

Answers

2. **1 mark for correct answer**
   500 × 9 = 4500 m and 4500 ÷ 1000 = 4.5 km
3. **1 mark for both correct**
   21 and 42
4. **1 mark for correct answer**
   Volume = L × W × H = 12 × 20 × 7 = 1680 cm³
   1680 cm³ is greater than 1500 cm³ so it would cost £3.00 to post the box.
5. **1 mark for correct answer**
   Angles on a straight line add up to 180°.
   So x = 180° − 130° = 50°
   1 mark for correct answer
   Angles in a triangle add up to 180° and it is an isosceles triangle so there are two 50° angles.
   So y = 180° − 50° − 50° = 80°
6. **1 mark**
   $\frac{4}{3} \times \frac{1}{10} = \frac{4}{30} = \frac{2}{15}$
7. **1 mark for correct answer**
   3 cm = 75 m, so 1 cm = 75 ÷ 3 = 25 m
   11 cm = 11 × 25 = 275 m
8. **1 mark for correct answer**
   25% of £40 = 40 ÷ 4 = £10
   75% of £40 = 10 × 3 = £30
   So he sold the game for £40 + £30 = £70
   1 mark for correct answer
   50% of £22 = 22 ÷ 2 = £11
   1% of £22 = 22 ÷ 100 = £0.22
   52% of £22 = 11 + 0.22 + 0.22 = £11.44

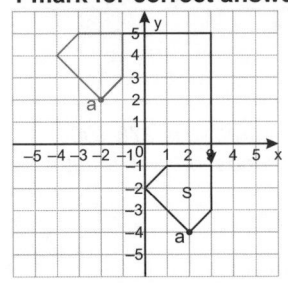

BONUS BRAINTEASER
She had 250 + 2 = 252 cards in total.
1 in 12 are rare cards, so do 252 ÷ 12.
$12 \overline{)2^2 5^1 2}$ = 21
She had 21 rare cards but she gave 2 away so she now has 21 − 2 = 19 rare cards.

Test 4 — pages 10-12

1. **1 mark for correct answer**
   309.4 × 9.6 ≈ 300 × 10 = 3000
   So the correct answer is 2970.24
2. **1 mark**
   ```
       3 6
     ×  2 4
     ─────
     1 4₂4
     7₁2 0
     ─────
     8 6 4
   ```
3. **1 mark**
   $\frac{5}{8} \div 3 = \frac{5}{24}$
4. **1 mark for correct answer**

   Point a: (2, −4).
5. **1 mark for correct answer**
   11 × 7 = 77 cm
   1 mark for correct answer
   630 mm = 63 cm, so x = 63 ÷ 7 = 9 cm
6. **1 mark for correct answer**
   D = 7 + (3 × 4) − 3 = 16 days
7. **1 mark for correct answer**
   $\frac{3}{4}$ of Ralph's ties are blue.
   $\frac{1}{4}$ of 36 = 36 ÷ 4 = 9, so $\frac{3}{4}$ of 36 = 9 × 3 = 27
8. **2 marks for correct answer**
   otherwise 1 mark for correct working
   The mean is 4 and there are 5 people, so the total number of guitars = 4 × 5 = 20.
   Ozzy must have 20 − 6 − 1 − 3 − 5 = 5 guitars

BONUS BRAINTEASER
$\frac{3}{4}$ of $\frac{6}{5}$ mm = $\frac{3}{4} \times \frac{6}{5} = \frac{18}{20} = \frac{9}{10}$ mm
The second string has a thickness of $\frac{9}{10}$ mm.
$\frac{3}{4}$ of $\frac{9}{10}$ mm = $\frac{3}{4} \times \frac{9}{10} = \frac{27}{40}$ mm
The third string has a thickness of $\frac{27}{40}$ mm.

Test 5 — pages 13-15

1. **1 mark for correct answer**
   $21 \overline{)4 4^4 8^6 3}$ = 23
2. **1 mark for correct answer**
   0.66 = $\frac{66}{100}$ and $\frac{13}{20} = \frac{65}{100}$
   So, 0.66 > $\frac{13}{20}$
3. **1 mark for both correct**
   The rule is 'multiply by 3 each time'. So the next two terms are: 27 × 3 = 81 and 81 × 3 = 243
4. **1 mark for correct order**
   $\frac{5}{6} = \frac{30}{36}$, $\frac{1}{2} = \frac{18}{36}$, $\frac{1}{4} = \frac{9}{36}$ and $\frac{4}{9} = \frac{16}{36}$,
   so the correct order is $\frac{5}{6}, \frac{1}{2}, \frac{4}{9}, \frac{1}{4}$

Answers

Answers

5. **1 mark for a correct net**
   E.g.

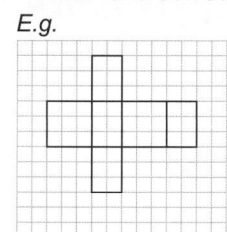

6. **1 mark for correct answer**
   5 miles ≈ 8 km, so multiply by 5, then divide by 8
   $44 \times 5 = 220$, $\frac{220}{8} = \frac{110}{4} = \frac{55}{2} = 27.5$ miles

7. **1 mark for correct shape L**

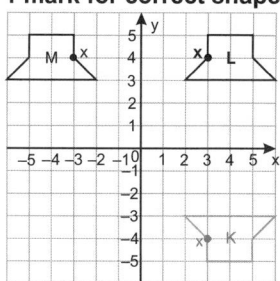

   1 mark for correct coordinate of x
   On shape M, x = (–3, 4)

8. **1 mark for correct answer**
   1 mark for some correct working
   Cafe A reduces the size of their drinks by
   $400 - 320 = 80$ ml, $\frac{80}{400} = \frac{40}{200} = \frac{20}{100} = 20\%$
   Cafe B reduces the size of their drinks by
   $300 - 225 = 75$ ml, $\frac{75}{300} = \frac{25}{100} = 25\%$
   Cafe B reduces the size of their drinks by the bigger percentage.

BONUS BRAINTEASER
The first digit must be a 0, 1 or 2.
The second digit is 0–9 if the first digit is a 0 or 1 or must be 0–3 if the first digit is a 2.
The third digit must be 0–5.
The last digit must be 0–9.
The only time it could show is 23:28

Arithmetic Test — pages 16-17

1. **1 mark**
   $-129 + 900 = 900 - 129 = 771$

2. **1 mark**
   $25.50 - 9.36 = 15.14$

3. **1 mark**
   $48 - 20 \times 2 = 48 - 40 = 8$

4. **1 mark**
   $135 \times 8 = 1080$
   135 is 100 times bigger than 1.35,
   so $1.35 \times 8 = 1080 \div 100 = 10.8$

5. **1 mark**
   $7^2 + 10 = 49 + 10 = 59$

6. **1 mark**
   10% of 350 = 350 ÷ 10 = 35
   30% of 350 = 35 × 3 = 105

7. **2 marks for correct answer**
   otherwise 1 mark for correct working
   $1341 \times 24 = 32184$

8. **2 marks for correct answer**
   otherwise 1 mark for correct working
   $4056 \div 13 = 312$

Set B

Test 1 — pages 19-21

1. **1 mark**
   $600\,909 = 600\,000 + 900 + 9$

2. **1 mark for correct answer**
   13 °C is the highest temperature. –4 °C is the lowest temperature. The difference between 13 °C and –4 °C is 13 + 4 = 17 °C

3. **1 mark**
   150 rupees
   1 mark
   6 euros

4. **1 mark for both correct**
   Mass of a scone: g
   Volume of a mug: ml

Answers

5. 1 mark

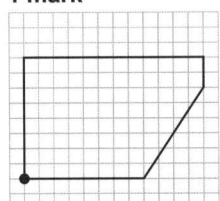

6. 1 mark for correct answer
If Jaden caught 3 × 4 = 12 butterflies then Louise caught 4 × 4 = 16 butterflies. So the total is 12 + 16 = 28.

7. 1 mark

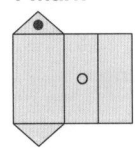

8. 2 marks for all correct pairs
otherwise 1 mark for at least one correct pair
The cost of the prizes needs to add up to 16 tokens, so 3t + 2d = 16.
(3 × 0) + (2 × 8) = 16, so t = 0, d = 8
(3 × 2) + (2 × 5) = 16, so t = 2, d = 5
(3 × 4) + (2 × 2) = 16, so t = 4, d = 2

BONUS BRAINTEASER
There are 18 hours from 3 am to 9 pm. If 11 bees enter and 3 bees leave every hour, the number of bees increases by 11 − 3 = 8 each hour. At 9 pm there will be 5 + (18 × 8) = 149 bees in the hive.

Test 2 — pages 22-24

1. 1 mark for both correct
7.643 and 7.638

2. 1 mark for correct answer
2 × 13 × 8 = 208 cm

3. 1 mark for both correct
$\frac{9}{36} = \frac{3}{12} = \frac{15}{60}$

4. 1 mark for correct answer
July and August each have 31 days, 31 + 31 = 62
```
    1 3
  ×  6 2
    2 6
  7₁8 0
  8 0 6
   ₁
```
She takes 806 photographs in total.

5. 1 mark

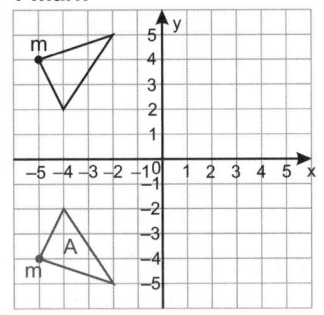

6. 1 mark for correct answer
Vertically opposite angles are equal so X + 90° = 147°, so X = 147° − 90° = 57°

7. 2 marks for correct answer
otherwise 1 mark for correct working
63% + 26% = 89%
10% of 1200 = 1200 ÷ 10 = 120
90% of 1200 = 120 × 9 = 1080
1% of 1200 = 1200 ÷ 100 = 12
89% = 90% − 1% = 1080 − 12 = 1068

8. 1 mark for correct answer
She does 240 ÷ 15 = 16 sets of steps, which means she does 16 × 5 = 80 star jumps.
1 mark for correct answer
She does 150 ÷ 5 = 30 sets of star jumps, which means she does 30 × 15 = 450 steps.

BONUS BRAINTEASER
For every 15 steps and 5 star jumps, she burns 1 + 1 = 2 calories. 70 = 2 × 35, so she does 15 × 35 = 525 steps to burn 70 calories.

Test 3 — pages 25-27

1. 1 mark for correct answer
```
    1 4 5
  ×     6
    8 7 0
     ₂ ₃
```
145 is 100 times bigger than 1.45, so £1.45 × 6 = £870 ÷ 100 = £8.70

2. 1 mark for correct answer
The factors of 27 are 1, 3, 9 and 27.
The factors of 45 are 1, 3, 5, 9, 15 and 45.
So the highest common factor is 9.

3. 1 mark for correct answer
$\frac{18}{40} = \frac{9}{20} = \frac{45}{100} = 45\%$

4. 1 mark for correct answer
53 × 3 = (50 × 3) + (3 × 3) = 150 + 9 = 159, so the next term will be 159 + 2 = 161.

Answers 58

Answers

5. **2 marks for correctly drawn shape otherwise
   1 mark for 3 sides and 2 angles correctly drawn**

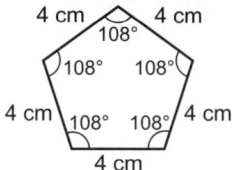

   (Pentagon with sides 4 cm and angles 108°)

6. **1 mark for correct answer**
   The new coordinates are (1 + 4, 5 − 8) = (5, −3)

7. **1 mark for correct answer**
   One part of water is 154 ÷ 11 = 14 ml
   Three parts of cordial is 3 × 14 = 42 ml

8. **1 mark for correct answer**
   $\frac{6 + 14}{4} = \frac{20}{4} = 5$
   1 mark for correct answer
   $\frac{4 + 14}{4} = \frac{18}{4} = \frac{9}{2} = 4.5$. Deeta needs a 4 to win.

BONUS BRAINTEASER
The dog moves 24 ÷ 2 = 12 m every second.
The cat moves 9 m every second, so the dog moves 12 − 9 = 3 m closer to the cat every second.
The dog will catch the cat in 27 ÷ 3 = 9 seconds.

Test 4 — pages 28-30

1. **1 mark for correct answer**
   $3 \overline{) 2\,^29\,^39}$ quotient 2 3... (1 3)

2. **1 mark for both correct**
   A: 12 × 4 = 48 cm², B: 5 × 9 = 45 cm²
   C: 7 × 8 = 56 cm², D: 8 × 6 = 48 cm²
   A and D have areas of 48 cm².

3. **1 mark for correct answer**
   8 × 11 − 47 = 88 − 47 = 41
   4 × 12 − 5 = 48 − 5 = 43
   36 + 20 ÷ 4 = 36 + 5 = 41
   98 − 7 × 7 = 98 − 49 = 49
   So 36 + 20 ÷ 4 should be circled.

4. **1 mark for correct answer**
   He has 100% − 64% = 36% left to do.
   $36\% = \frac{36}{100} = \frac{9}{25}$

5. **1 mark for correct answer**
   In week 6, 14 cars were sold.
   In week 7, 8 cars were sold.
   14 − 8 = 6 more cars were sold in week 6.
   **2 marks for correct answer
   otherwise 1 mark for correct working**
   5 + 20 + 7 + 11 + 5 + 14 + 8 = 70
   The mean number of cars sold is 70 ÷ 7 = 10.

6. **1 mark for correct answer**
   $2\frac{2}{3} - \frac{5}{6} = \frac{8}{3} - \frac{5}{6} = \frac{16}{6} - \frac{5}{6} = \frac{11}{6}$ or $1\frac{5}{6}$

7. **1 mark for both correct**
   Try multiples of 7 until you find the correct answer:
   6 × 7 = 42, 42 + 6 = 48,
   so the ticket numbers are 6 and 42.

8. **1 mark for correct answer**
   To get from (7, 5) to (4, 7) you subtract 3 from the x-coordinate and add 2 to the y-coordinate.
   To get from (4, 7) to P, you subtract 3 from the x-coordinate, then subtract 2 from the y-coordinate.
   So Point P is at (4 − 3, 7 − 2) = (1, 5)

BONUS BRAINTEASER
7, 13 and 23 are all primes. 7 + 13 + 23 = 43
23 − 7 = 16. So Louise's numbers are 7, 13, 23.

Test 5 — pages 31-33

1. **1 mark for correct answer**
   The radius of a circle is half of its diameter.
   52 ÷ 2 = 26 cm

2. **1 mark**
   $\frac{4}{13} \times \frac{5}{3} = \frac{20}{39}$

3. **1 mark for correct answer**
   5 miles ≈ 8 km. 2.5 miles ≈ 4 km,
   so 7.5 miles ≈ 8 + 4 = 12 km
   4.8 + 12 = 16.8 km

4. **1 mark**
   7 + 20 ÷ 4 = 12

5. **1 mark for a correct example**
   E.g. 2 is a prime number and (3 × 2) − 1 = 5, which is an odd number, so Louise is wrong.

6. **1 mark for correct answer**
   Sum of exterior angles = 360°, so each exterior angle in a regular decagon is $\frac{360}{10} = 36°$
   1 mark for correct answer
   Interior angle = 180° − exterior angle
   180° − 36° = 144°

7. **1 mark**
   5B + 2G + 5W
   **2 marks for correct answer
   otherwise 1 mark for correct working**
   (5 × 12) + 2G + 5W = 71
   60 + 2G + 5W = 71
   2G + 5W = 11
   (2 × 3) + (5 × 1) = 11, so G = 3 and W = 1.

Answers

BONUS BRAINTEASER

B	G	W
1	1	3
1	6	1
2	1	2
3	1	1

Arithmetic Test — pages 34-35

1. **1 mark**

   $6\ 8\ 7\ 2$
   $+\ \ \ 4\ 5\ 1$
   $\overline{7\ 3\ 2\ 3}$

2. **1 mark**

   $\ \ 2\ 3\ 1$
   $\times \ \ \ 9$
   $\overline{2\ 0\ 7\ 9}$

   231 is 10 times bigger than 23.1, so 23.1 × 9 = 2079 ÷ 10 = 207.9

3. **1 mark**

   $\frac{2}{5} \div 4 = \frac{2}{20}$ or $\frac{1}{10}$

4. **1 mark**

   120 × 12 ÷ 4 = 120 × 3 = 360

5. **1 mark**

   $4\frac{1}{3} = \frac{13}{3} = \frac{26}{6}$, $2\frac{5}{6} = \frac{17}{6}$

   $4\frac{1}{3} + 2\frac{5}{6} = \frac{26}{6} + \frac{17}{6} = \frac{43}{6}$ or $7\frac{1}{6}$

6. **1 mark**

   1% of 520 = 520 ÷ 100 = 5.2
   4% of 520 = 4 × 5.2 = 20.8

7. **2 marks for correct answer**
   otherwise 1 mark for correct working

   $\ \ 1\ 2\ 2\ 6$
   $\times \ \ 4\ 7$
   $\overline{8\ 5\ 8\ 2}$
   $4\ 9\ 0\ 4\ 0$
   $\overline{5\ 7\ 6\ 2\ 2}$

8. **2 marks for correct answer**
   otherwise 1 mark for correct working

   $\ \ \ \ 3\ 1\ 5$
   $19\overline{)5\ 9\ 8\ 5}$
   $-\ 5\ 7$
   $\ \ \ 2\ 8$
   $-\ 1\ 9$
   $\ \ \ 9\ 5$
   $-\ 9\ 5$
   $\ \ \ \ 0$

Set C

Test 1 — pages 37-39

1. **1 mark**

   $\ \ \ 5\ \ 4$
   $7\overline{)3\ ^37\ ^28}$

2. **1 mark**

   145 687

3. **1 mark for correct answer**

   Area of square = 10 × 10 = 100 cm²
   Area of triangle = $\frac{1}{2}$ × (16 − 10) × 10 = 30 cm²
   100 + 30 = 130 cm²

4. **1 mark for correct answer**

   X = 360° − 121° − 73° − 65° = 101°

5. **1 mark for correct answer**

   $\frac{1000}{8}$ = 125, so $\frac{1}{8}$ = 125 ÷ 1000 = 0.125

6. **1 mark for correct answer**

   $\frac{3}{4} + \frac{1}{7} = \frac{21}{28} + \frac{4}{28} = \frac{25}{28}$

7. **2 marks for all correct**
   otherwise 1 mark for at least one correct

   There are 12 segments on the pie chart.
   Each segment is worth 72 ÷ 12 = 6 people.
   Caravan = 4 × 6 = 24, Hotel = 5 × 6 = 30,
   Tent = 3 × 6 = 18

8. **2 marks for correct answer**
   otherwise 1 mark for correct length or width

   Multiply the length by 5, 15 × 5 = 75 cm, and the width by 3, 10 × 3 = 30 cm. So, the area of the enlarged rectangle is 75 × 30 = 2250 cm².

BONUS BRAINTEASER

You can make six two-digit prime numbers:
17, 41, 47, 61, 67, 71
You can make one two-digit cube number: 64

Test 2 — pages 40-42

1. **1 mark for correct answer**

   The difference between 18 °C and −11 °C is 18 + 11 = 29 °C.

   1 mark for correct answer

   To get from −56 to −89 you count 33 places.
   So the temperature difference was 33 °C.

2. **1 mark for correct answer**

   1.4 + 6.8 + 1.3 = 9.5 km

3. **1 mark for correct answer**

   The diameter of the second roll = 12 ÷ 2 = 6 cm
   The radius of the second roll = 6 ÷ 2 = 3 cm

Answers

Answers

4. **1 mark**
   3s = g

5. **1 mark for correct answer**
   Point P is 7 units right and 7 units down from (3, −1) = (3 + 7, −1 − 7) = (10, −8)

6. **1 mark for correct answer**
   10% of 160 = 160 ÷ 10 = 16,
   5% of 160 = 16 ÷ 2 = 8
   So they sold 160 + 16 + 8 = 184 albums.

7. **1 mark for correct answer**
   125 + 100 + 130 + 120 + 90 + 95 = 660 g
   660 ÷ 6 = 110 g

8. **2 marks for correct answer**
   otherwise 1 mark for correct working
   $2\frac{1}{4} = \frac{9}{4} = \frac{27}{12}$, $1\frac{7}{12} = \frac{19}{12}$, $\frac{2}{3} = \frac{8}{12}$
   So $2\frac{1}{4} - 1\frac{7}{12} + \frac{2}{3} = \frac{27}{12} - \frac{19}{12} + \frac{8}{12}$
   $= \frac{16}{12} = 1\frac{4}{12} = 1\frac{1}{3}$ or $\frac{4}{3}$ gallons

BONUS BRAINTEASER
The mean is 105 g, so the total weight of 8 onions is 105 × 8 = 840 g. From Q7, 6 onions weighed 660 g in total. 840 − 660 = 180 g, so each extra onion weighed 180 ÷ 2 = 90 g.

Test 3 — pages 43-45

1. **1 mark for correct answer**
   0.5 kg = 500 g. 500 ÷ 60 = 8 r 20.
   So he could fit a maximum of 8 eggs in the bag.

2. **1 mark for both correct**
   The sequence is adding 3 each time so:
   −4   −1   2   5   8   11   14

3. **1 mark for a correct explanation**
   1 + 2 + 3 + 4 + 5 + 6 + 7 = 28 is a triangle number.

4. **1 mark for correct answer**
   There are 11 + 6 + 7 = 24 packets in total.
   $\frac{6}{24} = \frac{1}{4}$ = 25% of packets are roast chicken.

5. **2 marks for all correct pairs**
   otherwise 1 mark for at least 2 correct pairs
   (3 × 1) + 8 = 11, so a = 1, b = 8
   (3 × 2) + 5 = 11, so a = 2, b = 5
   (3 × 3) + 2 = 11, so a = 3, b = 2

6. **1 mark**

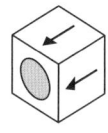

7. **1 mark for correct answer**
   Interior angle = 180° − exterior angle = 180° − 40°
   = 140°, so the sum of interior angles
   = 140° × 9 = 1260°.

8. **2 marks for correct answer**
   otherwise 1 mark for correct working
   Red and yellow apples make 4 + 3 = 7 shares.
   7 shares = 56 apples, so 1 share = 56 ÷ 7
   = 8 apples. Green apples make up 2 shares, so there are 8 × 2 = 16 green apples.

BONUS BRAINTEASER
Any correct net. E.g.

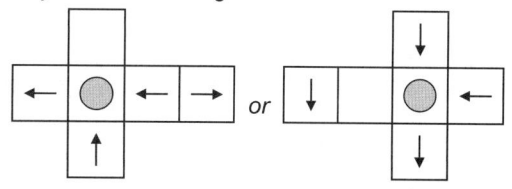

Test 4 — pages 46-48

1. **1 mark for correct answer**
   40 potatoes weigh 0.16 × 40 kg.
   0.16 × 10 = 1.6, 1.6 × 4 = 6.4 kg
   The sack weighs 0.4 kg, so the total weight of one sack of potatoes is 6.4 + 0.4 = 6.8 kg.

2. **1 mark**
   9 × 3 − 31 = −4

3. **1 mark for a correct explanation**
   Round (20.134 + 29.878) × 7.101 to
   (20 + 30) × 7 = 50 × 7 = 350.
   So Morag's answer, 206.132, is incorrect.

4. **1 mark for correct answer**
   Length of pattern: 20 + 10 + 10 + 10 = 50 cm
   Width of pattern: 10 + 10 + 20 = 40 cm
   Perimeter = 50 + 40 + 50 + 40 = 180 cm

5. **1 mark for correct answer**
   10% of 1300 = 1300 ÷ 10 = 130 g
   1% of 1300 = 1300 ÷ 100 = 13 g
   21% of 1300 = 130 + 130 + 13 = 273 g

6. **1 mark for correct answer**
   Volume of cuboid = 2 × 3 × 5 = 30 m^3
   Volume of stone = 30 − 12.36 = 17.64 m^3

7. **2 marks for correct answer**
   otherwise 1 mark for correct working
   £2.34 = 234p so each chocolate costs
   234 ÷ 18 = 13p
   Scott pays 13 × 23 = 299p = £2.99

Answers

8. **2 marks for correct answer otherwise 1 mark for correct working**

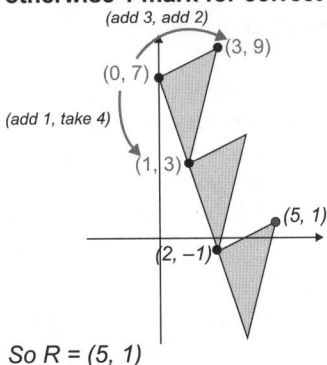

So R = (5, 1)

BONUS BRAINTEASER
6 ways: YRYB, YBYR, BYRY, RYBY, YBRY, YRBY

Test 5 — pages 49-51

1. **1 mark**

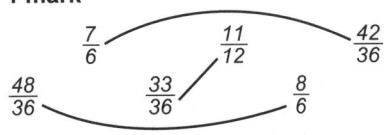

   $\frac{7}{6}$, $\frac{11}{12}$, $\frac{42}{36}$, $\frac{48}{36}$, $\frac{33}{36}$, $\frac{8}{6}$

2. **1 mark for all correct**
   154 ÷ 2 = 77, 77 ÷ 7 = 11
   So, 2 × 7 × 11 = 154

3. **1 mark for correct answer**
   Using vertically opposite angles, the angle between a and 30° is also 42°.
   So a = 180° − 30° − 55° − 42° = 53°

4. **1 mark for correct answer**
   There is 180 g of sugar in 400 g of jam, so 180 ÷ 2 = 90 g of sugar in 400 ÷ 2 = 200 g of jam, 90 × 5 = 450 g of sugar in 200 × 5 = 1 kg of jam
   1 mark for correct answer
   There is 40 g of grated lemon for every 180 g of raspberries, so 40 ÷ 4 = 10 g of grated lemon for 180 ÷ 4 = 45 g of raspberries, 10 × 5 = 50 g of grated lemon for 45 × 5 = 225 g of raspberries

5. **2 marks for correct answer otherwise 1 mark for correct rounding**
   20.219 − 3.675 + 4.234 rounds to
   20.2 − 3.7 + 4.2 = 20.7 kg

6. **1 mark for correct answer**
   Put the x-coordinate into the expression:
   (2 × 4) + 1 = 9. So the x-coordinate is 9.
   Put the y-coordinate into the expression:
   4 − (3 × 6) = −14. So the y-coordinate is −14.
   The coordinates of the moved counter are (9, −14).

7. **2 marks for correct answer otherwise 1 mark for correct working**
   The height of the kite is 22 cm so the height of each triangle is 22 ÷ 2 = 11 cm.
   Area of one triangle = $\frac{1}{2}$ × 40 × 11 = 220 cm^2
   Area of rectangle = 40 × 28 = 1120 cm^2
   Area of shaded area = 1120 − 220 − 220 = 680 cm^2

BONUS BRAINTEASER
The diameter of the black counter is 1 unit. The diameter of the white counter is 4 units as this is the distance from the right side (2, 0) to the left side (−2, 0). So the scale factor is 4 ÷ 1 = 4.

Arithmetic Test — pages 52-53

1. **1 mark**
   70 303 ÷ 1000 = 70.303

2. **1 mark**
   $\frac{3}{8} \div 6 = \frac{3}{48}$ or $\frac{1}{16}$

3. **1 mark**
   6^2 + (7 − 2)^2 = 36 + 5^2 = 36 + 25 = 61

4. **1 mark**
   10% of 800 = 80, 5% of 800 = 80 ÷ 2 = 40
   1% of 800 = 80 ÷ 10 = 8
   37% of 800 = 80 + 80 + 80 + 40 + 8 + 8 = 296

5. **1 mark**
   $3\frac{1}{7} = \frac{22}{7} = \frac{66}{21}$, $\frac{2}{3} = \frac{14}{21}$
   So $3\frac{1}{7} - \frac{2}{3} = \frac{66}{21} - \frac{14}{21} = \frac{52}{21}$ or $2\frac{10}{21}$

6. **1 mark**
   $2\frac{1}{3} = \frac{7}{3}$, $24 \times \frac{7}{3} = 8 \times 7 = 56$

7. **2 marks for correct answer otherwise 1 mark for correct working**
   ```
       4 5 2 6
   ×       3 9
     4 0 7 3 4
   1 3 5 7 8 0
   1 7 6 5 1 4
   ```

8. **2 marks for correct answer otherwise 1 mark for correct working**
   ```
           3 3 2
       27)8 9 6 4
          8 1
            8 6
          − 8 1
              5 4
            − 5 4
                0
   ```